Probing Deep Space

General Editor

William H. Goetzmann
Jack S. Blanton, Sr., Chair in History
  University of Texas at Austin

Consulting Editor

Tom D. Crouch
Chairman, Department of Aeronautics
  National Air and Space Museum
  Smithsonian Institution

WORLD EXPLORERS

Probing Deep Space

Terrance Dolan

Introductory Essay by Michael Collins

CHELSEA HOUSE PUBLISHERS

New York • Philadelphia

On the cover A star chart from *Uranographia*, a star atlas produced in 1802 by Johann Elert Bode; Spiral Galaxy NGC 2997.

Chelsea House Publishers
Editorial Director Richard Rennert
Executive Managing Editor Karyn Gullen Browne
Executive Editor Sean Dolan
Copy Chief Philip Koslow
Picture Editor Adrian G. Allen
Art Director Nora Wertz
Manufacturing Director Gerald Levine
Systems Manager Lindsey Ottman
Production Coordinator Marie Claire Cebrián-Ume

World Explorers
Senior Editor Sean Dolan

Staff for PROBING DEEP SPACE
Copy Editor Danielle Janusz
Editorial Assistant Robert Green
Picture Researcher Alan Gottlieb
Senior Designer Basia Niemczyc

5   7   9   8   6   4

Library of Congress Cataloging-in-Publication Data

Dolan, Terrance.
Probing Deep Space / Terrance Dolan; introductory essay #1 by Michael Collins: introductory essay #2 by William H. Goetzmann.
p. cm.—(World Explorers)
Includes bibliographical references and index.
Summary: Traces the history of deep space astronomy, from the early theories and discoveries of Copernicus, Kepler, and Galileo to recent research into quasars and extraterrestrial life.
ISBN 0-7910-1326-X
      0-7910-1550-5 (pbk.)
1.Space astronomy—History—Juvenile literature. [1. Astronomy.] I. Title.
II. Series.   92-25543
QB136.D65 1993   CIP
520—dc20   AC

CONTENTS

WORLD EXPLORERS

THE EARLY EXPLORERS

Herodotus and the Explorers of the Classical Age
Marco Polo and the Medieval Explorers
The Viking Explorers

THE FIRST GREAT AGE OF DISCOVERY

Jacques Cartier, Samuel de Champlain, and the Explorers of Canada
Christopher Columbus and the First Voyages to the New World
From Coronado to Escalante: The Explorers of the Spanish Southwest
Hernando de Soto and the Explorers of the American South
Sir Francis Drake and the Struggle for an Ocean Empire
Vasco da Gama and the Portuguese Explorers
La Salle and the Explorers of the Mississippi
Ferdinand Magellan and the Discovery of the World Ocean
Pizarro, Orellana, and the Exploration of the Amazon
The Search for the Northwest Passage
Giovanni da Verrazano and the Explorers of the Atlantic Coast

THE SECOND GREAT AGE OF DISCOVERY

Roald Amundsen and the Quest for the South Pole
Daniel Boone and the Opening of the Ohio Country
Captain James Cook and the Explorers of the Pacific
The Explorers of Alaska
John Charles Frémont and the Great Western Reconnaissance
Alexander von Humboldt, Colossus of Exploration
Lewis and Clark and the Route to the Pacific
Alexander Mackenzie and the Explorers of Canada
Robert Peary and the Quest for the North Pole
Zebulon Pike and the Explorers of the American Southwest
John Wesley Powell and the Great Surveys of the American West
Jedediah Smith and the Mountain Men of the American West
Henry Stanley and the European Explorers of Africa
Lt. Charles Wilkes and the Great U.S. Exploring Expedition

THE THIRD GREAT AGE OF DISCOVERY

Apollo to the Moon
The Explorers of the Undersea World
The First Men in Space
The Mission to Mars and Beyond
Probing Deep Space

CHELSEA HOUSE PUBLISHERS

Into the Unknown

Michael Collins

It is difficult to define most eras in history with any precision, but not so the space age. On October 4, 1957, it burst on us with little warning when the Soviet Union launched *Sputnik*, a 184-pound cannonball that circled the globe once every 96 minutes. Less than 4 years later, the Soviets followed this first primitive satellite with the flight of Yuri Gagarin, a 27-year-old fighter pilot who became the first human to orbit the earth. The Soviet Union's success prompted President John F. Kennedy to decide that the United States should "land a man on the moon and return him safely to earth" before the end of the 1960s. We now had not only a space age but a space race.

I was born in 1930, exactly the right time to allow me to participate in Project Apollo, as the U.S. lunar program came to be known. As a young man growing up, I often found myself too young to do the things I wanted—or suddenly too old, as if someone had turned a switch at midnight. But for Apollo, 1930 was the perfect year to be born, and I was very lucky. In 1966 I enjoyed circling the earth for three days, and in 1969 I flew to the moon and laughed at the sight of the tiny earth, which I could cover with my thumbnail.

How the early explorers would have loved the view from space! With one glance Christopher Columbus could have plotted his course and reassured his crew that the world was indeed round. In 90 minutes Magellan could have looked down at every port of call in the *Victoria*'s three-year circumnavigation of the globe. Given a chance to map their route from orbit, Lewis and Clark could have told President Jefferson that there was no easy Northwest Passage but that a continent of exquisite diversity awaited their scrutiny.

In a physical sense, we have already gone to most places that we can. That is not to say that there are not new adventures awaiting us in the sea or on the red plains of Mars, but more important than reaching new places will be understanding those we have already visited. There are vital gaps in our understanding of how our planet works as an ecosystem and how our planet fits into the infinite order of the universe. The next great age may well be the age of assimilation, in which we use microscope and telescope to evaluate what we have discovered and put that knowledge to use. The adventure of being first to reach may be replaced by the satisfaction of being first to grasp. Surely that is a form of exploration as vital to our well-being, and perhaps even survival, as the distinction of being the first to explore a specific geographical area.

The explorers whose stories are told in the books of this series did not just sail perilous seas, scale rugged mountains, traverse blistering deserts, dive to the depths of the ocean, or land on the moon. Their voyages and expeditions were journeys of mind as much as of time and distance, through which they—and all of mankind—were able to reach a greater understanding of our universe. That challenge remains, for all of us. The imperative is to see, to understand, to develop knowledge that others can use, to help nurture this planet that sustains us all. Perhaps being born in 1975 will be as lucky for a new generation of explorer as being born in 1930 was for Neil Armstrong, Buzz Aldrin, and Mike Collins.

The Reader's Journey

William H. Goetzmann

This volume is one of a series that takes us with the great explorers of the ages on bold journeys over the oceans and the continents and into outer space. As we travel along with these imaginative and creative journeyers, we share their adventures and their knowledge. We also get a glimpse of that mysterious and inextinguishable fire that burned in the breast of men such as Magellan and Columbus—the fire that has propelled all those throughout the ages who have been driven to leave behind family and friends for a voyage into the unknown.

No one has satisfactorily explained the urge to explore, the drive to go to the "back of beyond." It is certain that it has been present in man almost since he began walking erect and first ventured across the African savannas. Sparks from that same fire fueled the transoceanic explorers of the Ice Age, who led their people across the vast plain that formed a land bridge between Asia and North America, and the astronauts and scientists who determined that man must reach the moon.

Besides an element of adventure, all exploration involves an element of mystery. We must not confuse exploration with discovery. Exploration is a purposeful human activity—a search for something. Discovery may be the end result of that search; it may also be an accident, as when Columbus found a whole new world while searching for the Indies. Often, the explorer may not even realize the full significance of what he has discovered, as was the case with Columbus. Exploration, on the other hand, is the product of a cultural or individual curiosity; it is a unique process that has enabled mankind to know and understand the world's oceans, continents, and polar regions. It is at the heart of scientific thinking. One of its most significant aspects is that it teaches people to ask the right questions; by doing so, it forces us to reevaluate what we think we know and understand. Thus knowledge progresses, and we are driven constantly to a new awareness and appreciation of the universe in all its infinite variety.

The motivation for exploration is not always pure. In his fascination with the new, man often forgets that others have been there before him. For example, the popular notion of the discovery of America overlooks the complex Indian civilizations that had existed there for thousands of years before the arrival of Europeans. Man's desire for conquest, riches, and fame is often linked inextricably with his quest for the unknown, but a story that touches so closely on the human essence must of necessity treat war as well as peace, avarice with generosity, both pride and humility, frailty and greatness. The story of exploration is above all a story of humanity and of man's understanding of his place in the universe.

The WORLD EXPLORERS series has been divided into four sections. The first treats the explorers of the ancient world, the Viking explorers of the 9th through the 11th centuries, and Marco Polo and the medieval explorers. The rest of the series is divided into three great ages of exploration. The first is the era of Columbus and Magellan: the period spanning the 15th and 16th centuries, which saw the discovery and exploration of the New World and the world ocean. The second might be called the age of science and imperialism, the era made possible by the scientific advances of the 17th century, which witnessed the discovery of the world's last two undiscovered continents, Australia and Antarctica, the mapping of all the continents and oceans, and the establishment of colonies all over the world. The third great age refers to the most ambitious quests of the 20th century—the probing of space and of the ocean's depths.

As we reach out into the darkness of outer space and other galaxies, we come to better understand how our ancestors confronted *oecumene*, or the vast earthly unknown. We learn once again the meaning of an unknown 18th-century sea captain's advice to navigators:

> And if by chance you make a landfall on the shores of another sea in a far country inhabited by savages and barbarians, remember you this: the greatest danger and the surest hope lies not with fires and arrows but in the quicksilver hearts of men.

At its core, exploration is a series of moral dramas. But it is these dramas, involving new lands, new people, and exotic ecosystems of staggering beauty, that make the explorers' stories not only moral tales but also some of the greatest adventure stories ever recorded. They represent the process of learning in its most expansive and vivid forms. We see that real life, past and present, transcends even the adventures of the starship *Enterprise*.

Childhood's End

The need to understand the stars, and to understand our place among them, has propelled humankind on its most profound journey of discovery. "I take on wings of light and soar through all spaces of the heavens," wrote the 18th-century astronomer Johann Lambert. "I never go far enough and the desire always grows to go still farther . . ."

For a long time, humans looked at the skies and concluded that we live in a small, domed cosmos, intimate and cozy, much like today's planetariums, where the stars and planets dapple a low, gently curved ceiling; one might reach up and touch them with the help of some sturdy scaffolding. It was believed that the earth was cradled at the center of this starry room like a fetus nurtured in a mother's womb, and that all the celestial bodies circled our planet like doting relatives. Early astronomers and cosmologists came to these conclusions by studying the perceived motions of the stars and planets, the moon and the sun. *Motion*—the movements of the celestial bodies in relation to each other and in relation to the earth—was the foundation on which astronomy was built.

Humankind's perception and understanding of the cosmos has progressed in great, giddy leaps and bounds since then. Astronomy as it is practiced today, on the cusp of the millennium, has evolved from the study of motion to the study of *light*. Once content to ponder the familiar motions of the moon and the planets, astronomers now scrutinize the light from quasars that sparkle like fiery diamonds at the very edge of the universe. And yet, today's astronomers and cosmologists are asking of the night skies essentially

Italian scientist Galileo Galilei (1565–1642), the father of deep-space astronomy. Galileo embodied the two aspects of cosmology that still hold true today—theory and observation. He used both to show that the sun, not the earth, is at the center of the solar system. Persecuted for this and other assertions by the Roman Catholic church, Galileo declared that "by denying scientific principles, one may maintain any paradox."

A Ptolemaic, or geocentric, portrait of the universe. A stationary earth, resting at the center of the cosmos, is orbited by the sun, the moon, the planets, and the zodiac constellations.

the same questions that yesterday's astronomers and cosmologists asked. The quest continues for what the 16th-century cosmologist Nicolaus Copernicus called "the principal thing—namely the shape of the universe and the unchangeable symmetry of its parts." What has changed, and dramatically so, is our point of view. We no longer perceive the earth as being the stationary centerpiece of a relatively small universe, the hub of a friendly planetary neighborhood. Instead, we now know that it is but a tiny speck of matter hurtling through space on the outskirts of a galaxy of a billion stars that is but a speck itself in a universe of a billion galaxies. This change in our point of view began with the Copernican revolution.

Before Nicolaus Copernicus arrived on the scene—he was born in Poland in 1473—the prevailing *cosmology* (a cosmology is a theory of the structure and nature of the cosmos, or universe) was based on a *geocentric* (earth-centered) model. The bible of geocentricity was *Almagest* (Arabic for "The Greatest"), written by the Greco-Egyptian mathematician, geographer, and astronomer Claudius Ptolemy sometime around A.D. 125. Ptolemy based much of his cosmology on the theories of the classical Greek philosophers and astronomers, such as Eudoxus and Aristotle.

In the Ptolemaic cosmos, as defined in *Almagest*, the earth resided, motionless, at the center of the universe; the sun, moon, planets, and stars orbited the earth, and the planets also completed separate little circular journeys, called epicycles, during their primary journey around the earth. With this system, Ptolemy explained—and in many cases was able to predict—the observed motions of the celestial bodies across the skies, and the Ptolemaic model of the cosmos became widely accepted as scientific doctrine. And because it was consistent with the official views of the Roman Catholic church concerning the origin and nature of the cosmos and placed earth and humanity at the center of the universe, where both the church and most scientists believed we rightfully belonged, the Ptolemaic model (in Christian Europe at least) eventually became firmly entrenched religious dogma as well.

By 1543, the year in which Copernicus published his *De Revolutionibus* (On the Revolutions), the work that was to eclipse Ptolemy's *Almagest*, the Catholic Church, ruled by the pope from Rome, was the single most powerful social and political force in Europe. Rome wielded its power with a heavy hand. Dissenters, including astronomers who made claims that were not in line with the teachings of the church, were persecuted, and sometimes executed, as heretics.

It is not surprising, then, that Copernicus was a reluctant revolutionary. The Polish astronomer kept his model of the cosmos—which explained the motions of the celestial bodies by placing a rotating earth, and the other planets as well, in orbit around the sun, and the moon in orbit around the earth—hidden away until shortly before his death in 1543.

The revolution fomented by the publication of *De Revolutionibus* and its *heliocentric* (sun-centered) model of the cosmos was a rather quiet one at first. It was characterized by a gradual erosion of geocentricity, as astronomers, over the years, began to see the merits of the Copernican system.

The 2nd-century astronomer and mathematician Claudius Ptolemy, author of Almagest, *the accepted cosmological treatise for more than 1,400 years. Ptolemy based much of* Almagest *on the theories of the ancient Greek astronomers. "We shall only report what was rigorously proved by the ancients," Ptolemy wrote.*

The Polish astronomer Nicolaus Copernicus (1473–1543). A furtive cosmological subversive, Copernicus wrote De Revolutionibus, *his "ballet of the planets," in secrecy, fearing religious persecution.* De Revolutionibus *was the work that was to eventually undermine geocentrism. "In the center," wrote Copernicus, "is the sun."*

Few astronomers were inclined to directly challenge the church over this issue; most were content to quietly adopt the heliocentric model as a guide to their own work. The fireworks did not begin until 1623, a full 80 years after the discreet Copernicus had slipped away.

Galileo Galilei was the Babe Ruth of astronomy—a larger-than-life character, impossibly gifted and more than willing to let people know about it. Born in Pisa in 1564, he was a true Renaissance man. No other single figure in the history of science—except, perhaps, Sir Isaac Newton—has excelled in so many different disciplines or made such vital contributions in so many different fields, from philosophy to physics to optics to astronomy. His intellect was immense, his energies prodigious. He courted public recognition and fame—as well as controversy—and by the time he was 45 he was widely thought to be the most brilliant man in Europe, the dinner guest of cardinals and kings, a star of the first magnitude. With his encyclopedic brain and rapier-sharp writing and speaking skills, Galileo, a staunch heliocentrist, was just the man to take up the standard of Copernicanism—or so he thought.

Despite his widespread popularity and his formidable intellectual powers (and despite the fact that he was right), Galileo was playing a dangerous game. In 1600, the Italian philosopher and astronomer Giordano Bruno was brought before the Inquisition—the church body responsible for rooting out heresy—in Rome for his public espousal of Copernicanism. Bruno, a true visionary, had also asserted that the universe contained untold numbers of suns and planets. Convicted of blasphemy and heresy, Bruno was ordered to recant on pain of death. He refused and was burned at the stake.

Although Galileo was certainly aware of the fate of Bruno and although he was warned by friends within the Vatican—"This is no place to come to argue about the moon," he was told—he nevertheless published, in 1623, *The Assayer*, a witty, sarcastic, and often scathing attack on the Ptolemaic model of the cosmos. Because a friend of his had just been elected pope (Urban VIII), Galileo was spared any reprisal from Rome. But in 1632, Galileo published another pro-Copernican work, *Dialogue . . . Concerning the Two Chief World Systems, Ptolemaic and Copernican*. In this work, it was quite evident that the great scientist and philosopher was attempting to make a monkey out of the Vatican. This would not do.

Galileo Galilei, now 70 years old, was summoned to Rome. There, he was interrogated by the Jesuit cardinal Roberto Bellarmino, a fearsome inquisitor known as "the hammer of the heretics." Galileo was fighting a losing battle by this point, for whether or not the earth turned or the sun was at the center of the cosmos was immaterial to the pope and Bellarmino; this was a matter of the authority of the church. The earth was at the center of the cosmos, Bellarmino asserted. It did not rotate, and it was orbited by the sun and the planets. Galileo, on his knees, under threat of torture and no doubt thinking about Giordano Bruno, saw no choice but to retract his own opinions, and that was that. (Legend has it, however, that as he left the room the scientist muttered under his breath, in reference to the earth, "And yet it moves.")

Like a wayward schoolboy, Galileo was then sent to his room—for the rest of his life. He spent his last years under house arrest at his villa near Florence. At night he would lean out an upstairs window, peering at the sky with a telescope, cursing the pope and his own failing eyesight. But if Galileo had lost the battle, he would win the war, for the Copernican cat was out of the bag. Other astronomers, such as the Dane Tycho Brahe and the brilliant German Johannes Kepler, had not only embraced Copernicanism but were in the process of improving on it, correcting its deficiencies, and eventually making it irrefutable. The idea that the earth was at the center of the universe was fading like a cherished but whimsical notion of childhood. Feeling much less certain about the importance of the earth in the overall cosmological scheme of things, the astronomers of the 17th century turned their attention to the stars and deep space. The lesson in humility had begun.

(In October 1992, almost 360 years after Galileo's persecution and after more than three and a half centuries of extensive inquiry into the question on the part of the Roman Catholic church, Pope John Paul II declared that the Vatican's position on the heliocentric solar system was officially in accordance with Galileo's Copernican theories.)

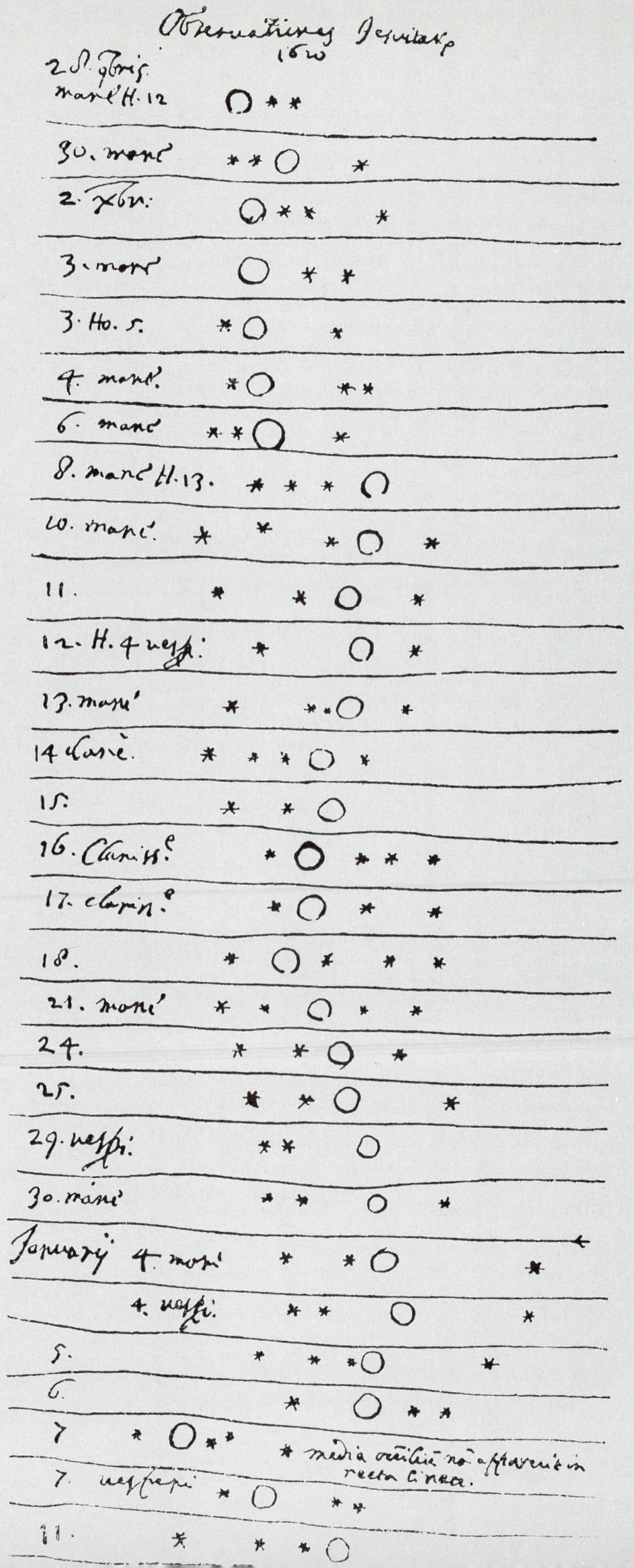

Obſervationeſ Jeſuitarp
1610

2 d. 9bris:
mane H. 12   ○ * *

30. mane   * * ○   *

2. xbr: ○ * *   *

3. mane   ○ * *

3. Ho. 5.   * ○   *

4. mane.   * ○   * *

6. mane   * * ○   *

8. mane H. 13.   * * * ○

10. mane.   *   *   * ○   *

11.   *   * ○   *

12. H. 4 veſp: *   ○   *

13. mane   *   * * ○   *

14 veſp̀e.   *   * * ○   *

15.   *   * ○

16. Clariſſ.ᵉ   * ○ * *   *

17. clariſ.ᵉ   * ○   *   *

18.   * ○ *   *   *

21. mane   *   *   ○   *   *

24.   *   * ○   *

25.   *   * ○   *

29. veſpi: * *   ○

30. mane   *   * *   ○   *

Januarÿ 4. mane   *   * ○   *

     4. veſpi.   * *   ○   *

5.   *   * * ○   *

6.   *   ○   * *

7   * ○ * *
              *   media occulta nõ apparuit in
                     recta linea.

7. veſperi   * ○   * *

11.   *   *   * ○

Galileo's Ladder, or A Short History of Long Telescopes

Just as the history of the exploration of the seas and oceans of the world is linked inextricably to the history of sailing vessels, the history of the exploration of deep space cannot be separated from the history of the telescope. Nobody is quite sure who invented the first telescope, although it is known that these devices originally appeared in Holland at the beginning of the 17th century. According to one account, a Dutch spectacle grinder named Hans Lippershey noticed that if he lined up two lenses and looked through them both at once they made faraway objects appear closer. He then put them in a tube to make them easier to look through, creating a telescope. Other Dutch lens makers then began to build telescopes of their own.

Back in Italy, Galileo Galilei, who had not yet run afoul of the Vatican, and who seems to have had a hand in everything, heard about these new devices. Immediately grasping the optic principles involved, he built one of his own. Then he built a few more, each one more powerful than the last. In 1609, when he had designed one that "enlarged objects more than 60 times," he did something that nobody else had yet thought to do—he took it outside at night and pointed it at the sky.

Galileo's record of the movements of the planet Jupiter and 4 of its many moons (it has at least 16). Jupiter, the fifth planet from the sun, was one of the first celestial objects Galileo studied through a telescope. Soon after, he turned the instrument to the stars, thus becoming the first deep-space astronomer.

With his telescope—soon dubbed "Galileo's ladder" by one of his contemporaries—Galileo looked at the moon, then he looked at Jupiter, and then he aimed it at the soft splash of light known as the Milky Way. What he saw was a revelation: "You will behold through the telescope a host of other stars, which escape the unassisted sight, so numerous as to be almost beyond belief. The Milky Way . . . is, in fact, nothing but a congeries of innumerable stars grouped together in clusters. Upon whatever part of it the telescope is directed, a vast crowd of stars is immediately presented to view. Many of them are rather large and quite bright, while the number of smaller ones is quite beyond calculation." Galileo Galilei had discovered outer space.

But Galileo's "ladder" was an imperfect one: a refracting telescope. Refracting telescopes use a curved lens to gather and magnify light, and the simple lenses of the 17th century, as many astronomers soon noted, created a prism effect, causing distortions of color called chromatic aberrations. Galileo, his attention and energy taken up by other matters, never got a chance to improve on his model. In 1667, 25 years after Galileo's death, the problem fell into the hands of the master English mathematician Sir Isaac Newton.

When he was not busy formulating his theory of universal gravitation, Newton liked to observe comets and planets through a refracting telescope. Annoyed by the shortcomings of this instrument (nobody wants to look at a *blue* Mars), Newton built a better one—the reflecting telescope. The reflecting telescope uses a curved mirror instead of a curved lens to collect light. Newton placed a concave mirror in the back end of the telescope tube and viewed the light gathered by the mirror through a magnifying eyepiece at the front end. Because a mirror does not cause color distortions, the reflecting telescope eliminated chromatic aberration and presented to the eye a sharper, more focused image.

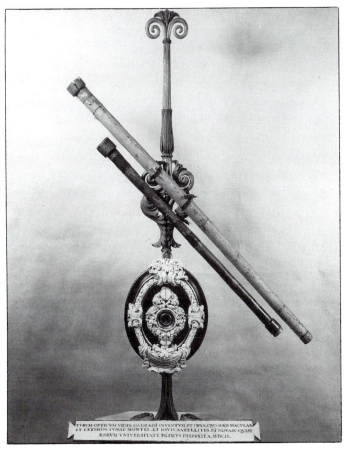

TVBVM OPTICVM VIDES GALILAEI INVENTVM,ET OPVS,QVO SOLIS MACVLAS
ET EXTIMOS LVNAE MONTES ,ET IOVIS SATELLITES,ET NOVAM QVASI
RERVM VNIVERSITATE PRIMVS DISPEXIT A. MDCIX.

One of Galileo's refracting telescopes. In the final years of his
life, under house arrest by the
Vatican, Galileo used such a telescope to peer out an upper window
at the stars at night. In 1637, he
went blind. "This universe that I
have extended a thousand times,"
he lamented, "has now shrunk to
the narrow confines of my own
body."

But the true importance of the reflecting telescope was
its potential light-gathering power. The larger the surface
of the mirror, the greater the light-gathering capability.
(The relation is proportional; a mirror twice the size of
another mirror can gather four times as much light, and so
on.) The greater the light-gathering capability, the deeper
into space a telescope can "see." Although Sir Isaac was no
doubt aware of the ultimate potential of his invention (he
was aware of everything), he left the realization of this
potential to others—he was a busy man. Almost a century
passed before the next rungs were added to Galileo's ladder.
In the interim, astronomers seemed content to use the
small telescopes that were available, perhaps because these

telescopes, despite their limitations, still gave them plenty to look at.

It was a musician who eventually took up the task of exploring the deep-space potential of the reflecting telescope. In 1756, a friendly, intelligent young man named William Herschel found himself wandering about war-torn Europe. The Seven Years' War was raging, and Herschel, a musician, was playing oboe in an army band. He decided that the battlefield was no place to play the oboe and fled to England. His engaging personality and his talents as a musician won him a multitude of friends and admirers in London society, and by the age of 30 he had acquired a prestigious position as organist for the Octagon Chapel in Bath.

Herschel's position at the Octagon Chapel left him a lot of free time. He spent much of it reading—Herschel was a tireless, avid reader who was frequently seen riding his horse about town while deeply engrossed in some book— and one of his favorite topics was astronomy. Tired of simply reading about the stars, he rented a small reflecting telescope—they were fairly common by that time—and began spending his nights reading the heavens. He soon came to the conclusion, much like Galileo and Newton, that he could build a better telescope himself, which he presently did. Then he built several more, each with a larger mirror. With each new mirror, he saw increasing numbers of stars. At night, he could be found in his backyard at 19 New King Street in Bath, sweeping the sky with his latest telescope. He would stay out until dawn, no matter what the weather (as long as it was not overcast), studying the stars and planets and recording their positions in what he called his "Book of Sweeps."

In 1781, Herschel decided to build a telescope with a 36-inch-diameter mirror. A concave mirror of that size could not be had anywhere, so Herschel made plans to cast one himself. Short on funds, he built the mold for his mirror out of a singularly inexpensive material—horse manure.

Aided by his sister Caroline and a friend, he shaped the pungent mold in his basement. Once the mold had dried sufficiently, he carried it out to his yard and poured in the molten metal for the mirror. The mold broke apart under the intense heat, and Herschel and his assistants were chased by a river of lava onto a pile of bricks. When the liquid metal reached the bricks, they began to heat up and then explode, and the three would-be mirror builders cowered atop the little island while shrapnel flew about the yard. Herschel was reminded unpleasantly of his oboe-playing days in the army.

Fortunately for Herschel (and for his sister, friends, and neighbors), the king of England, George III, had been made aware of Herschel's accomplishments as an astronomer, which included the discovery of the planet Uranus. Herschel was given a fellowship in the prestigious Royal Society and was also granted the money he needed to build his big telescope. A team of craftsmen, under Herschel's supervision, constructed the world's largest telescope—a behemoth of a telescope, with a 48-inch, 2,000-pound mirror housed within a 40-foot tube. On the night that the telescope was unveiled, the king, along with various members of the Royal Society and other dignitaries, watched as Herschel climbed a 50-foot ladder and peered into the telescope's eyepiece. Then he climbed back down and wandered away, apparently stunned. "I have looked," he was heard to say, "farther into space than any human being did before me."

Herschel had pushed 18th-century technology to its limits; indeed, he had pushed it past its limits, for his telescope, and the other big reflecting telescopes built during the following century, were too unwieldy to be of much practical use. (Herschel himself continued his stellar career using mostly smaller telescopes, mapping the sky right up until his death at the age of 82, in 1821.) By the beginning of the 20th century, the technology to build larger and more viable reflecting telescopes existed, but by then Herschel was long gone. What was missing now was somebody with Herschel's vision and ambition. Not surprisingly, this person appeared in America, the land of big ideas and big money to see them through. His name was George Ellery Hale, and he was the father of that union of high finance and high technology that would come to be known as Big Science.

Born in 1868, George Ellery Hale was the product of a moneyed New England family. A Rhodes scholar and a gifted astronomer, Hale was obsessed with the idea of building reflecting telescopes with mirrors big enough

William Herschel (1738–1822), musician, astronomer, and telescope builder. Herschel built a series of telescopes of unprecedented size. His largest had a 40-inch mirror in a 40-foot tube. The telescope and its supporting equipment was described by Oliver Wendell Holmes as "a mighty bewilderment of slanted masts, spars and ladders and ropes, from the midst of which a vast tube lifted its muzzle towards the sky."

George Ellery Hale (1868–1938), the father of "Big Science" astronomy. Hale was obsessed with building bigger and better telescopes, and he sometimes worked so frantically that he suffered nervous breakdowns. The breakdowns were often heralded by the appearance of a hallucinatory "little man," who would sit at the foot of Hale's bed and offer him unwanted advice.

to allow astronomers to see farther into space than they ever had before. The secrets of deep space awaited humanity, Hale believed, and telescopes with great, big, American-sized mirrors would unveil those secrets. Subsequently, Hale began displaying a remarkable talent for convincing very wealthy men to spend huge sums of their money on gigantic telescopes.

Shortly after the turn of the century, Hale convinced his father and steel baron Andrew Carnegie to finance the construction of a 60-inch reflecting telescope on Mount Wilson, near Pasadena, California. (Size designations for reflecting telescopes always refer to the diameter of the mirror.) It was completed in 1908 and was the largest reflector on earth until 1918, when it was surpassed by a

Engineers at work on Hale's 100-inch Hooker telescope, situated atop Mount Wilson in Southern California. Hale was not yet satisfied, however. "Starlight is falling on every square mile of the earth's surface," he commented, "and the best we can do is gather up the rays that strike an area 100 inches in diameter."

100-inch monster, paid for, at the behest of the persuasive Hale, by a California hardware magnate named John Hooker. The Hooker telescope, also situated atop Mount Wilson, was soon attracting some of the world's most distinguished astronomers, and the initial forays into true deep space had begun. But Hale was not finished. He dreamt of building a bigger telescope, twice as large as the Hooker, an instrument equipped with a massive, 200-inch mirror. Millions of dollars would be needed for this. Hale contacted John D. Rockefeller in 1929, and plans were drawn up for the construction of what is still considered to be the greatest reflecting telescope ever built.

Nobody in the mirror-making business had ever considered casting a 200-inch mirror, and many experts thought it could not be done, but the project began nevertheless in 1934 at the Corning Glass Works in Corning, New York. A mold was built and then filled with 42,000 pounds of white-hot liquid Pyrex. (Herschel would have been delighted.) It took 10 months for the Pyrex to cool and solidify. The glass disk was then lifted from the mold, encased in a steel shell, and transported in an upright position, via railroad flatcar, across the United States. The train moved at a crawl for fear the glass would be disturbed. Armed guards were stationed on the flatcar. Large crowds lined the railway to look at the object, as if it were a captured flying saucer. When the train arrived in Pasadena on April 10, 1936, bands played and the crowd

The mold for Hale's 200-inch mirror, cast at the Corning Glass Works in Corning, New York. The 14-ton mirror that was formed within the mold was the world's largest piece of glass.

that had gathered at the station cheered. The great disk remained in the station overnight, bathed in the glow of floodlights. The next day it was transported to the optical shop at the California Institute of Technology (also known as Caltech).

Under the direction of Marcus Brown, Caltech's head optician, the polishing of the glass began. Using everything from jeweler's rouge to motor oil to ground-up walnut shells, the opticians, dressed in white, polished the disk as it rotated on a specially designed turntable. They polished day in and day out. Years went by. The men in white continued to polish. Opticians left for new jobs; other opticians took their place at the spinning disk. By 1941,

Dedication of the 200-inch Hale telescope in January 1949, 15 years after the project had begun. The tube is seven stories tall, and the mirror itself is stabilized by 36,000 support units. The Hale telescope is still considered the most sensitive telescope on earth.

five and a half tons of glass had been polished away and the surface of the disk had assumed a concave shape. The opticians continued polishing, for the surface had to be honed to a parabolic accuracy of one-half of one-millionth of an inch in order to correctly focus starlight. World War II broke out and the project was halted. When the war ended, those opticians who had survived returned to Caltech and continued polishing. Finally, in 1947, the disk was placed inside a vacuum chamber, and thin aluminum wires were vaporized over the surface of the glass, giving it a layer of aluminum with the precise thickness of 1,000 atoms. The disk was now a mirror.

George Hale was long dead by this time, but before he died he had picked out the site for the great telescope—Palomar Mountain in southern California. There, in a meadow 5,000 feet above sea level, the dome that would house the telescope was built—a replica of the Roman Pantheon with a slit in the dome for the telescope. In 1948, the mirror was brought up the mountain and placed at the base of a 55-foot tube, which was cradled by a gigantic rotating yoke that looked like the world's largest tuning fork. On the night of January 26, 1949, in a ceremony known as First Light, a select group of astronomers—including a man named Edwin Hubble—looked into the telescope. "I had never seen so many stars in my life," one of them remembered later. "It was like pollen on a fish pond." Fittingly, the telescope was named after George Ellery Hale, but to this day, astronomers refer to it as the Big Eye.

Aldebaran and Betelgeuse

The ever-improving telescopes of the 17th, 18th, and 19th centuries allowed astronomers to see more stars, and to see them more closely. Bigger, better telescopes were on the way. Techniques such as parallax, or triangulation, provided astronomers with the first rough estimates of distances between the earth and the growing numbers of stars they were seeing through their telescopes. (*Parallax* is a method of measuring the distance of a celestial body from the earth by sighting its apparent position against background stars from two or more separate locations.) But these instruments and techniques could not tell astronomers what the stars *were*; what they were made of; what made them shine. Most astronomers theorized that the stars were gaseous bodies of some kind, perhaps much like our own sun, but without any real scientific data, they were limited to speculation. The stars remained, in a sense, as inscrutable and untouchable as they had seemed to the ancient civilizations that attributed godlike qualities to them. "We understand [the celestial bodies'] shapes, their distances, their sizes and motion, whereas never, by any means, will we be able to study their chemical composition" lamented the French philosopher Auguste Comte in 1835.

Enter the astrophysicists with their spectroscopes. *Astrophysics* is the branch of astronomy concerning the physical and chemical makeup of stars and other celestial matter. It is practiced exclusively through the examination of the light—visible light as well as nonvisible electromagnetic

Like Galileo, an astronomer turning a telescope toward the Milky Way might be rewarded with a view such as this. As telescopes improved, astronomers began to question what these celestial bodies were made of.

radiation—emanated by celestial objects. The primary instrument of the astrophysicist is the spectroscope, which has proved to be as important as the telescope to the exploration of deep space.

The first astrophysicist, not surprisingly, was Sir Isaac Newton. In 1666, Newton placed a prism in the path of a ray of sunlight that penetrated into a darkened room. The

Sir Isaac Newton (1642–1727), remembered best for his theory of universal gravitation and his invention of the calculus, was also the first scientist to conduct experiments in astrophysics. Newton's immense intellect has been equaled by no one in the history of science except for Albert Einstein; his biographer Richard Westfall, who spent fully 20 years writing an account of Newton's life, concluded that he was "a man not fully reducible to the criteria by which we comprehend our fellow beings."

prism refracted, or broke up, the light, dividing it into a spectrum—a band of colors, ranging from red at one end of the spectrum to orange, yellow, green, and then violet at the other end, much like a rainbow. What Newton had done was to divide sunlight, a form of electromagnetic radiation, into its constituent wavelengths, which the human eye sees as colors. But Newton, apparently, was no more interested in the implications of this phenomenon than he had been in the potential uses of reflecting telescopes, and he pursued the matter no further. A century and a half passed before the phenomenon of the spectrum was investigated more fully and the science of astrophysics was truly born.

In 1802, English physicist William Wollaston placed a barrier between a ray of incoming sunlight and a prism. There was a tiny slit in the barrier. The sunlight that passed through the slit and into the prism was divided up so sharply that dark lines appeared at intervals along the spectrum. Wollaston's crude device was in fact the first spectroscope. Galileo's ladder allowed humans to climb into deep space and look closely upon the stars; Wollaston's device would eventually allow humans to stand upon the ladder and examine the very stuff the stars were made of.

We know today that the dark lines that Wollaston saw in his spectrum were absorption lines, caused by the absorption of light of certain wavelengths by the presence of the atoms of various elements in the sun's outer layers. For Wollaston, however, the lines were a mystery. Twelve years later, a Bavarian optician named Joseph Fraunhofer built a better spectroscope, which focused, then divided, and then refocused light as it passed through a slit, then through a lens, then a prism, and then another lens. Using his spectroscope to examine sunlight, Fraunhofer saw hundreds of absorption lines. Like Wollaston, he was mystified by this phenomenon. He pondered the enigma until his death in 1826, but he could not break the code of the dark lines. (continued on page 38)

All Things Must Pass

According to the ancient Greek philosophers, the stars were "fixed and immutable," the constant, changeless, and immortal inhabitants of the heavens, appearing nightly in all their brilliance and beauty, yet forever unknowable. But the stars are, in fact, neither fixed, immutable, or unknowable. Like humans, they are born, they live and change, they grow old, and they die—it just takes them a long time to do so. Some stars have lifespans of millions of years, others hundreds of millions, and still others billions of years. Inevitably, however, they all burn out and shine no longer.

What is a star? George Ellery Hale, who was an influential solar astronomer as well as a builder of telescopes, was often heard to declare happily, "The sun is a star!" delighted that one of these miraculous objects had been placed in such close proximity to the earth for the benefit of people like himself. And indeed, when we look at the sun, we are favored with an up-close view of one of the estimated billion billion stars that inhabit the universe.

A star is a super-hot (our sun is 27,000,000 degrees Fahrenheit at its core), massive ball of gas. Words such as "massive" quickly lose their impact when discussed on a cosmological scale, but in relative terms, a star is certainly massive; if the earth was a marble, for example, the sun would be a basketball. Our sun is an average if somewhat smallish star in the white-yellow color range. (The various colors, and luminosities, or magnitudes, of the stars as seen from earth, are the result of a combination of interrelated factors, especially a star's temperature, which in turn is determined by its mass and age. Generally speaking, hotter stars range toward blue in color, whereas cooler stars are reddish, with the whitish-yellowish stars like our sun falling in between the two extremes.)

Stars are created when vast interstellar clouds of gas and dust, called nebulae, come together through gravitational attraction. As this matter coalesces, a protostar—a loose, globular mass of the stuff—results. Gravitational forces cause the protostar to condense and heat up. Eventually, the contraction causes tremendous pressure and heat in the core of the protostar, igniting a process of fusion reaction in which hydrogen, the most abundant element in the protostar (and in the universe) is converted to helium. This process causes the protostar to "switch on," to begin radiating energy—to shine.

When the protostar's energy output equals the pressure exerted on it by gravity, a balance is achieved and the protostar stabilizes and stops contracting. The protostar is now a star; in effect, a gigantic thermonuclear reactor in outer space. It now enters what is known as the main sequence, the prime of a star's life, burning hydrogen and radiating energy steadily. A star remains in its main sequence for about 80 percent of its lifetime. (Our sun, which is an estimated 5 billion years old, is smack in the middle of its main sequence.)

Inevitably, however, a star exhausts its supply of hydrogen fuel. Its outer layers begin to cool, and the star swells tremendously and turns red, becoming what is known as a red giant. (A red giant is aptly named; 5 billion years or so down the road, when our sun enters the red giant phase, it will engulf our entire solar system.) Star death comes in a variety of forms: the red giant may become unstable and explode violently in a supernova; or it may simply collapse, becoming a kind of fading stellar cinder, known as a white dwarf, or a small, cold, burned-out black dwarf. A star that was originally very large may undergo profound gravitational collapse, resulting ultimately in a superdense stellar core known as a neutron star or forming that most enigmatic of celestial occurrences—a black hole.

The granular appearance of the photosphere, or visible outer surface, of the sun. The outer layers of stars such as our sun consist of a photosphere; a chromosphere, the solar atmosphere just above the photosphere; and a corona, the outermost region of the sun's atmosphere.

(continued from page 35)

The mystery was solved in 1861. Two German physicists, Gustav Kirchhoff and Robert Bunsen, began using spectroscopes to study the spectra of various chemical elements in their laboratory. They observed that, when heated, each element displayed a distinctive pattern of dark lines in its spectrum. Kirchhoff and Bunsen turned their spectroscope to the sun, and, like detectives examining sets of fingerprints, they began comparing the spectra of laboratory elements to the sunlight's spectrum. They found matching patterns of dark lines, indicating among other things, the presence of magnesium, iron, and chromium in the sun. For the first time, humans knew, at least in part, what a stellar body was made of.

The implications of this discovery were staggering, and it did not take long for other astronomers and physicists to react. News of the breakthrough "came to me like the coming upon a spring of water in a dry and thirsty land," wrote London-based astronomer William Huggins. Feeling, perhaps, the same excitement Galileo felt as he pointed his telescope at the night sky for the first time, Huggins attached a spectroscope to a telescope and pointed it at two stars, Aldebaran and Betelgeuse. Their spectra revealed the presence of various elements, including iron and magnesium. The stars, it seemed, were made of some of the same elements that were found in the earth and the sun. Suddenly, the stars were no longer the utterly alien

Dark lines in the spectrum of the star O Ceti reveal that the star consists of the elements hydrogen, helium, and iron. The numbers next to the hydrogen (H) lines indicate electron-energy transitions within the hydrogen atoms.

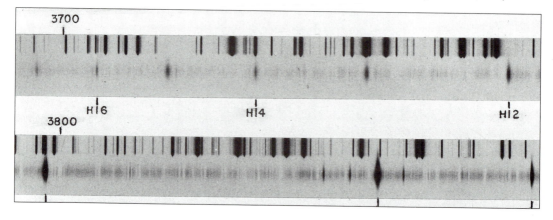

3700

HI6   HI4   HI2

3800

objects they had always seemed to be, and astronomers no longer had to content themselves with merely looking at them and wondering what glowing secrets these celestial bodies harbored. In the years to come, as astronomers moved ever deeper into space, the astrophysicists would travel along with them—much like the botanists and geologists who traveled with the nautical explorers of the 18th and 19th centuries—using their spectroscopic instruments and techniques to dissect and analyze the increasing numbers of stars and the other, far stranger objects encountered along the way.

Harlow Shapley Dances on the Stars

The first half of the 20th century witnessed an expansion of cosmological awareness that would prove to be as profound as the conceptual revolution brought about by the theories of Copernicus and the invention of the telescope. With this expansion of awareness would come additional lessons in cosmological humility, for the more humankind learned about the universe, the more insignificant their home planet appeared to be. As astronomers and astrophysicists probed deep space, the universe grew steadily bigger, while the earth seemed to shrink, eventually attaining the status of a grain of sand in a very large desert.

At the outset of the 20th century, advances in spectroscopy were providing new insights into the stars; astronomers were beginning to understand more fully not only the physical make-up of stars, but their origins and life cycles as well. Big reflecting telescopes—especially those built by George Ellery Hale—were allowing astronomers to see farther and farther into space, and hence to see objects they had never seen before. New methods of determining deep-space distances were being developed and perfected. And, with the aid of the emerging technology of photography, stars by the thousands were being captured on film and catalogued.

The globular cluster Omega Centauri. Globular clusters are gravitationally bound groups of hundreds of thousands of stars. Many of these clusters, which played such an important role in the exploration of the Milky Way, can be viewed with a decent pair of binoculars.

Most early 20th-century astronomers—with three centuries of astronomical observation to fall back on—believed that the earth's solar system resided at the center of a system of thousands and perhaps millions of stars known as the Milky Way galaxy. (The term *galaxy* comes from the Greek word for milk, *gala*. Galaxy, roughly translated, means "like milk," a reference to the Milky Way's appearance as viewed from earth.) This conceit echoed, on a much larger scale, the old geocentric, pre-Copernican view of the cosmos, placing the earth, once again, at the relative center of things. Like geocentrism, it was a belief that was to be rudely shattered.

In 1914, George Ellery Hale recruited a young astronomer named Harlow Shapley to come to California and work with the 60-inch telescope on Mount Wilson. (Hale was already making plans for the 100-inch Hooker telescope; the 200-inch mirror was still just a glimmer in his eye.) Shapley, a confident and ambitious Missourian, traveled to California, hiked up the mountain to the observatory (a nine-mile trek), and went to work. Initially, Shapley's goal was, as he put it, "to get distances."

The first distance ever calculated for a star had been obtained by Friedrich Bessel in 1837. Bessel, using a method known as stellar parallax, had determined that the star 61 Cygni was 523,000 astronomical units away from earth; an astronomical unit (AU) was the average distance between the earth and the sun—about 93 million miles. People were astounded at Bessel's claim for 61 Cygni. Such vast distances were almost incomprehensible.

Things had changed since then, though people were still equally astounded at stellar distances, if not more so. By the beginning of the Hale era, Bessel's 61 Cygni was considered a *local* star. After Bessel, astronomers had continued to measure stellar distances, reaching deeper and deeper into space, finding stars farther and farther away from earth, and the only limits they had yet encountered were on their own resources for carrying out such measurements with accuracy. The AU was no longer the yardstick for celestial distances. Now the light-year was the standard unit of measure. Light travels at 186,000 miles per second—the greatest speed that can be attained by any material particle or energy flow in the known universe. (The speed of light was determined by Albert Michelson in 1879.) A light-year is thus the distance light travels in a year—about 6 trillion miles. The closest star to earth is Alpha Centauri, which is 4.3 light-years away. Bessel's 61 Cygni is 10.9 light-years away.

By the time Harlow Shapley arrived at the Mount Wilson Observatory, astronomers had obtained distances for stars more than 100 light-years away from earth, but they

Harlow Shapley, the man who first mapped the shape and size of our home galaxy, the Milky Way, and determined the location of our solar system within it. A latter-day Copernicus, Shapley announced that "the solar system can no longer maintain a central position [within the Milky Way]."

had given up using triangulation methods to calculate stellar distances; these methods were not accurate for objects beyond about 90 light-years. Astronomers were now using the visible characteristics of the stars themselves to determine how far away they were. This was a tricky, heady game, involving intense observations and subtle comparisons of the varying positions, sizes, colors, and luminosities of stars. Shapley was something of a virtuoso at this pursuit, a masterful improviser and innovator. Up on Mount Wilson, he began using recently discovered Cepheid variable stars as "standard candles," or comparative distance indicators. (Cepheid variables are gigantic pulsating stars whose luminosity, or magnitude, increases and decreases regularly and dramatically, making them easy to locate and relocate amid the stellar multitudes.) Shapley began to "get distances" indeed. He leaped from one Cepheid milestone to another, adding on the distances as he climbed into galactic space, a Missouri-born Jack scaling a stellar beanstalk. In this manner, peering night after night through the 60-inch Mount Wilson telescope, pushing the instrument to its limits, young Shapley traveled hundreds, and then thousands of light-years away from earth, shattering his own distance records nightly. He eventually found himself wandering starstruck among the globular clusters.

The globular clusters are basically what the name indicates—dense globs of hundreds of thousands of stars. There are about 100 of them visible from earth, glowing on the very outskirts of the Milky Way. Shapley began to map them, moving from cluster to cluster. A pattern emerged: the clusters were distributed in a great sphere. Shapley realized that the globular clusters formed, in his own words, "a sort of framework—a vague skeleton of the whole Galaxy." As he mapped the clusters, Shapley was able to discern the shape and relative size of the Milky Way—a flat disk hundreds of thousands of light years across. And Shapley had even more startling news: According to his

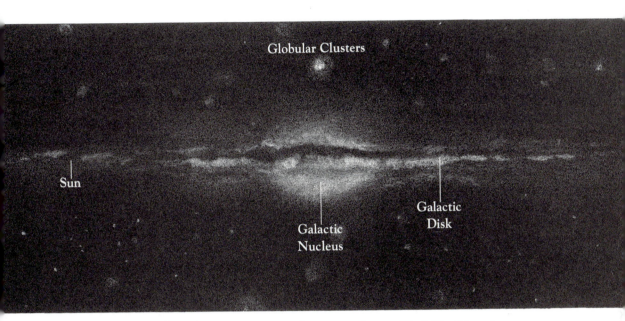

The Milky Way galaxy.

galactic map, the earth's solar system was nowhere near the center of the Milky Way. Instead, it appeared to be located about 30,000 light-years away from the center, out in the galactic boondocks along what today's astronomers know as one of the Milky Way's spiral arms.

Once Shapley's fellow astronomers had digested this humbling bit of information, they began asking the inevitable question: What—if anything—lay beyond Shapley's galactic outposts, the globular clusters? "Nothing," was Shapley's answer. He believed that the Milky Way was the entire universe, that the clusters marked its perimeter, and that he, Shapley, was the first man to see the edge of the cosmos. This point of view came to be known as the "big galaxy hypothesis." Many astronomers agreed with Shapley. Certainly, they argued, the Milky Way seemed big enough to comprise the entire universe; they were now speaking in terms of hundreds of thousands of light-years—godlike distances, or so it seemed. And nothing had yet been seen beyond the globular clusters. But other astronomers were not so sure. What about the spiral nebulae? they asked.

The spiral nebulae were bright but somewhat fuzzy spiral shaped celestial "objects" that astronomers had been arguing about for centuries. Most astronomers believed that these nebulae were clouds of gas that lay well within the confines of the galaxy, an idea that Shapley endorsed because he believed that there was *nothing* beyond the Milky Way's perimeter. But other, more radical astronomers believed that the spiral nebulae were themselves galaxies—great disks of stars much like the Milky Way but located far, far away from the Milky Way across an intergalactic gulf. This was a startling—and to some, an overwhelming—idea, considering the recent revelations about the size of the Milky Way. (It was not an astronomer who first suggested this theory but rather the great 18th-century philosopher Immanuel Kant. In 1750, Kant, then 26 years old, published a slim volume entitled *Universal Natural History and Theory of the Heavens*, in which he theorized that the spiral nebulae were in fact galaxies, islands of stars in a vast cosmic ocean.)

The spiral nebulae became the focus of an all-encompassing controversy concerning deep space and the very structure and nature of the universe. Harlow Shapley, who had outdone Copernicus in displacing the earth, now found himself defending his own "conservative" cosmology against advocates of Kant's "island universe" theory. Both sides knew that if the mystery of the spiral nebulae could be solved, the larger question would be answered as well. What was needed, clearly, was a *really big* telescope, one that was powerful enough to definitively resolve a spiral nebula into a cloud of gas or a collection of stars.

Right on cue, in 1918 George Ellery Hale unveiled his latest marvel—the Hooker telescope with its 100-inch mirror. The Hooker telescope was also built atop Mount Wilson, where it loomed like an ogre over its 60-inch little brother. There it stood, a mile above Los Angeles, like a great ship waiting for a captain bold enough to take its helm and guide it out through the dense Milky Way to the globular clusters and, perhaps, beyond.

The man who was to take on that job certainly had all the right characteristics. Edwin Hubble seemed able to do anything. He was physically and intellectually imposing. A Rhodes scholar, a star basketball player at the University of Chicago, a light-heavyweight boxer with championship potential, an attorney, and a gifted astronomer as well, he gave the unmistakable impression that he was a man who did not suffer fools lightly; and indeed he did not. His admirers called him brilliant; his rivals—Shapley among them—called him arrogant (but not to his face). In 1920, Hubble returned from World War I. At the invitation of Hale, who courted him like a big-league baseball owner might court a .400 hitter, Hubble came to Mount Wilson and took the helm of the Hooker telescope. While Shapley continued to staunchly defend his big-galaxy hypothesis and while a giddy Hale turned his thoughts toward building an even bigger telescope, Hubble trained the Hooker on the Andromeda spiral nebula.

Hubble took photograph after photograph of the Andromeda nebula as seen through the big telescope. He focused and tinkered with the Hooker, the camera, and the photographic plates, and took more pictures. By 1923, he had resolved the nebula into what appeared to be "dense swarms of . . . ordinary stars." But Shapley argued that the photographs were inconclusive; the "stars," he asserted, were probably nothing more than some kind of optical effect produced by the emulsions Hubble was using on his photographic plates. Hubble continued taking pictures of the Andromeda nebula through the Hooker telescope, but now he began comparing all the photographic plates with one another. In early 1924, he found what he was looking for: one of the "stars" in his photographs became brighter than all the others for a successive number of plates, then faded, then glowed brighter again. It was a Cepheid variable, flashing like a beacon across the immense blackness of intergalactic space. This was no optical effect; it was a star, undeniably a star, situated within the Andromeda nebula. And where there was one star there were, Hubble correctly assumed, invariably millions of others.

Hubble sent a brief note to Shapley. "You will be interested to hear," Hubble wrote, "that I have found a Cepheid variable in the Andromeda Nebula." Reading this, Shapley no doubt felt that a large crack had appeared in his big galaxy. And indeed, Shapley's galaxy could not hold Hubble's universe. Applying the same methods Shapley

Edwin Hubble, the greatest astronomer of the 20th century, peers through the eyepiece of the 48-inch Schmidt telescope on Palomar Mountain. At the time of his death in 1953, Hubble was studying the most distant visible galaxies in an attempt to measure the actual curvature of the universe so as to determine if the universe was "open" (expanding forever) or "closed" (eventually slowing its expansion and coming to a halt).

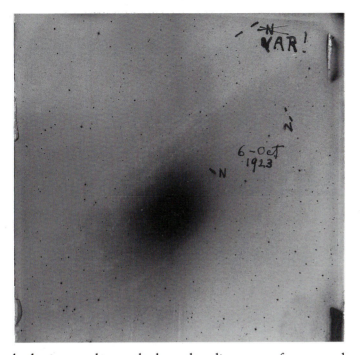

The photographic plate that originally revealed a Cepheid variable star in the disputed Andromeda nebula, proving it to be a galaxy outside the Milky Way rather than a gaseous cloud within the Milky Way. Hubble has scrawled the date of the discovery and "VAR!," for variable star, on the plate.

had pioneered to calculate the distances of stars and globular clusters, Hubble determined that the Cepheid variable in the Andromeda galaxy was at least *one million* light-years away, well beyond the globular clusters and thus well outside the confines of the Milky Way. (Recent estimates place the Andromeda galaxy about 2.2 million light-years away from the earth.) During the following years, using improved photographic techniques developed by self-made photoastronomer Milton Humason (who got his start in astronomy as the janitor at the Mount Wilson Observatory), Hubble continued to resolve the previously blurry spiral nebulae into distinct galaxies—brilliant stellar islands, as Immanuel Kant had predicted, in the vast cosmic ocean. By the time the 200-inch Hale telescope went on line in 1948, Hubble and other astronomers had seen that there were thousands of galaxies; the Hale telescope, with Hubble and then Alan Sandage at the helm, would reveal hundreds of millions more, some of them billions of light-years away from earth.

Abbé Lemaître's Fourth of July

W hile Shapley and Hubble were redefining the size and structure of the universe, a theoretical physicist named Albert Einstein was redefining the laws by which it was governed. Einstein, a gentle-natured German Jew with a soon-to-be-famous, tangled bird's nest of hair and a pair of puppy-dog eyes, published his special theory of relativity in 1905 and his general theory of relativity in 1916. Einstein's general theory electrified the scientific world. The eminent German physicist Max Born declared that it was "the greatest feat of human thinking about nature, the most amazing combination of philosophical penetration, physical intuition, and mathematical skill. It appeals to me like a great work of art."

To say that Einstein's theories revolutionized physics is an understatement; they actually revolutionized human-kind's perception of the very nature of reality. For more than 200 years, Sir Isaac Newton's classical physics—especially his law of universal gravitation—had stood as the rock-solid foundation of physical science. All motion in the cosmos, from falling apples to moons orbiting planets, was thought to be governed by Newtonian physics. Einstein's physics offered a view of a different reality. For example, in Newton's universe, gravity was interpreted as a force of attraction between two objects. In Einstein's universe, gravity was instead caused by grooves in *space-time*. (According to relativity, space-time is the actual fabric of the physical universe, a four-dimensional

The Andromeda galaxy, also known as Messier 31, the closest spiral galaxy to the Milky Way. Although they are almost 3 million light years apart, Andromeda and the Milky Way are gravitationally bound "sister galaxies" locked in an orbital dance.

continuum having three dimensions of space and one of time.) Grooves or warps in space-time were formed by the presence of concentrations of matter, such as planets and stars. According to classical Newtonian physics, an apple fell to earth because objects of a larger mass (the earth), attracted objects of a lesser mass (an apple). In Einstein's physics, on the other hand, the apple "rolled" or "slid" to earth down an incline in space-time caused by the presence of the earth.

Deep-space astronomy in the first decades of the 20th century was becoming increasingly dominated by radical concepts of space, time, and energy and thus proved to be a particularly well-suited arena for the observation of some of general relativity's more dramatic manifestations. In 1917, while investigating some of these manifestations (with pencil and paper; Einstein rarely looked through a telescope), Einstein discovered that according to his theory, the universe was either expanding or contracting. Here was a truly mind-boggling idea. Einstein himself was so unnerved by it that he assumed he had made a mistake in the equations that supported the general theory. His attempts to reconcile general relativity to the principle of a static universe sent him off on a mathematical wild-goose chase. The conundrum would not be resolved until evidence that the universe was indeed expanding began to arrive from deep space.

The man on the receiving end of this information was Edwin Hubble. Hubble, still up on Mount Wilson, was now sailing through vast archipelagoes of galaxies millions of light years away. In 1928, while using a spectroscope along with the Hooker telescope to examine light from the most distant galaxies yet observed, Hubble discovered a curious thing. The spectra from these galaxies were redshifted.

A *redshift* is the displacement toward the lower frequency, or red end of the spectrum, of the light coming from a star, galaxy, or other celestial object. A *blueshift*, conversely, is a shift toward the higher frequency, or blue end of the

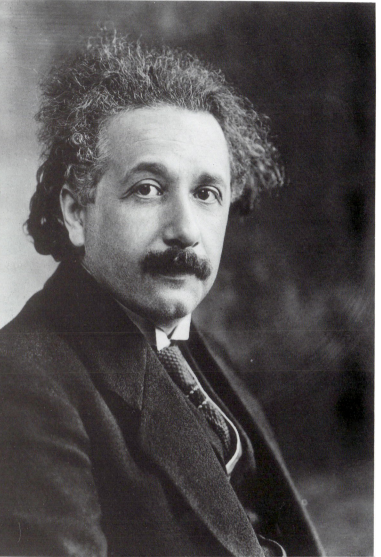

Albert Einstein. When Einstein discovered that his general theory of relativity implied a universe that was either expanding or contracting, he found the idea so unappealing that he added an artificial value—the "cosmological constant"—to his equations to eliminate the phenomenon. But even Einstein could not make the universe stand still, and he later called the cosmological constant "the worst blunder of my life."

spectrum, of such light. Both phenomena are types of *Doppler shift*, discovered by the Austrian physicist Christian Johann Doppler in 1842. A Doppler shift in the light received from a celestial body tells an astronomer whether that object is moving toward or away from earth. If the light is blueshifted, the object is coming toward earth. If the light is redshifted, it is moving away from earth. The degree of redshift or blueshift will also tell the astronomer the relative velocity at which the object is moving toward or away from earth.

Hubble, analyzing the spectra of 25 of the most distant galaxies, found that they were redshifted. The redshifts indicated that the galaxies were receding at unheard-of velocities. Hubble also discovered that the more distant the galaxy, the more deeply redshifted its light was. In other

In 1929, Edwin Hubble observed that 25 of the most distant galaxies yet seen were receding at phenomenal velocities. This discovery led to the conclusion that the universe is expanding. Today it is known that all galaxies that are not gravitationally bound are flying out and away from all other galaxies.

words, the farther away the galaxy, the faster it was receding. This correlation would come to be known as the Hubble law, or Hubble's constant, and, as Hubble soon noted, it held true for all galaxies observed in deep space. The universe, it seemed, was expanding, and at a phenomenal rate.

Hubble did not yet know much about Einstein or his general theory of relativity, and he had never heard anything about Einstein's non-static universe dilemma. Nor had Einstein learned of Hubble's discovery. Hubble published his galactic redshift findings in 1929, but, perhaps a bit overwhelmed by their potential significance—he later would admit only that his discovery was "rather startling"—he declined to speculate on their cosmological ramifications. Einstein, apparently, did not read about Hubble's finding. Soon, however, other physicists who were applying relativity to cosmology—primarily stellar physicist Sir Arthur Eddington of England and a Belgian priest and astrophysicist named Georges-Henri Lemaître—had made the connection between Hubble's observations and Einstein's theory. The word spread. Hubble learned of Einstein's expanding universe "problem," and Einstein learned of Hubble's redshift observations. With great relief—and great annoyance at himself for having doubted his own theory—Einstein dropped his mathematical attempts to maintain a static universe. Hubble, who was now credited with making one of the greatest discoveries in the history of science, remained as stoic as always and continued his nightly voyages among the galaxies.

Einstein and Hubble finally met in the flesh in 1931 at the Mount Wilson Observatory. Hubble gave Einstein, who was by then the world's most celebrated scientist, a tour of the facility. During the momentous visit, the disheveled and ever-amiable Einstein cracked jokes with the onetime janitor Milton Humason, who was by then recognized as something of a wizard in the field of photoastronomy. In the meantime, the universe continued expanding and Abbé Lemaître, back in Brussels, continued to think about that fact.

In person, Georges-Henri Lemaître was a short, stout, unassuming fellow. When he attended gatherings of physicists and astronomers, he was usually overlooked, and in the presence of luminaries such as Einstein, Hubble, and Eddington, he became virtually invisible. But as an astrophysicist and cosmologist, Lemaître could shine like the brightest of stars. He was capable of astounding theoretical leaps, and as he pondered the concept of an expanding universe, Lemaître made one of those leaps.

It was, in a sense, a leap backward. If the universe was expanding, Lemaître reasoned, there must have been a moment when the expansion began. If one followed the idea of universal expansion in reverse to its logical, ultimate point of origin, one found all the matter and energy in the universe condensed into a single mass. Lemaître called this original nucleus of matter and energy the "primeval atom." Today's astrophysicists refer to it as a *singularity*—a profoundly concentrated point of matter and energy. (Singularities resulting from collapsed stars are believed to be the sources of black holes.) Some physicists believe that Lemaître's singularity may have been as small as a *quark*—the smallest known subatomic particle.

In Lemaître's singularity could be found all the matter and energy in the universe, squeezed into a tiny point of maximum density. According to the principles of general relativity, such a dense concentration of matter would warp the space-time continuum infinitely; the gravity of the singularity would be so profound that it would wrap the space-time continuum around itself, allowing no outward flow of space, matter, energy, or time. According to Lemaître's theory, time began, and the universe as we know it was created, when the singularity—for reasons as yet unknown—exploded violently. This was the moment of creation. Lemaître imagined the explosion as a kind of cosmic Fourth of July, with "fireworks of unimaginable

beauty." Today, this event is known to cosmologists—and to everybody else—as the Big Bang. The violence of the Big Bang, Lemaître contended, was so intense that the universe was still flying apart, or expanding, as Hubble's redshifted galaxies testified.

Reactions to Lemaître's Big Bang theory were varied. Some physicists and astronomers were enraptured by it. Einstein called it "very, very beautiful." The dour Hubble, despite the role his work played in the formulation of the theory, found it to be a bit melodramatic for his tastes. Sir Arthur Eddington echoed Hubble's sentiments, condemning the Big Bang scenario as "too unaesthetically abrupt." Many scientists were put off by the Big Bang theory because

From left to right are physicists R. A. Millikan, Abbé Georges Lemaître, and Einstein. It was said of Lemaître, one of the pioneers of the Big Bang theory, that as far as physics were concerned, "symmetry was nearly as important as truth."

it seemed to be more theology than science, a reservation
that was given added weight when the Roman Catholic
church officially endorsed the Big Bang as being consistent
with Vatican doctrine, no doubt causing Giordano Bruno
and Galileo to turn in their graves. (Lemaître, at least, saw
no problem there; he was often heard to say, "There is no
conflict between science and religion.")

Astronomers and physicists on both sides of the argu-
ment began searching for ways to prove or to disprove the
Big Bang hypothesis. One of them was George Gamow, a
Russian nuclear physicist who had defected to the United
States in 1933. (Gamow had first attempted to flee Stalinist
Russia by paddling a rubber raft across the Black Sea to

*Nuclear physicist George Gamow
believed he could discover what
happened during the first seconds
of the Big Bang by studying the
relative abundance of atomic elements in the universe. His study
led to the proposal that the Big
Bang, if it occurred, would have
left behind a cosmic background
radiation.*

Turkey. The physicist and his wife set out from Odessa but were caught in a violent storm. They survived the storm, but when it lifted, they found that they had been washed back to their point of origin. They made a more successful and less risky defection shortly thereafter during a physics conference in Brussels.)

One of the first scientists to link the study of atomic and nuclear physics to the study of astrophysics, Gamow interpreted the Big Bang as a kind of thermonuclear explosion—the granddaddy of all thermonuclear explosions. According to his calculations, such an explosion would have left behind a certain amount of residual energy, a kind of afterglow, the fading warmth of what was once a great heat. This afterglow, according to Gamow, would exist in the form of a persistent, low-level "hiss" of microwave radiation that would have no apparent source, and that would be present throughout the universe. At the time, however, there were no instruments sensitive enough to detect this background radiation, if it indeed existed, and Gamow's theory was temporarily forgotten as astronomers turned their attention to other matters—including the discovery and exploration of the invisible universe, an entire cosmos that existed just outside the range of human vision.

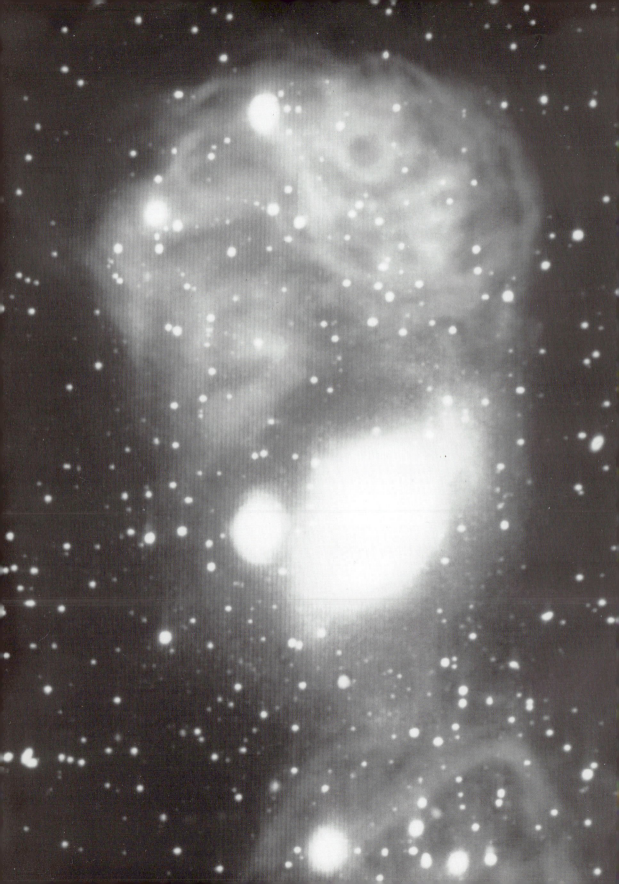

Jansky's Sky

The invisible universe was discovered in 1932. The initial discovery occurred in a potato field in New Jersey, of all places. Carl Jansky, a Bell Telephone employee working at Bell's Crawford Hill facility in Holmdel, New Jersey, had been assigned the task of investigating the static that interfered with transatlantic telephone communications, which had been initiated in 1927 by AT&T. Jansky, an enterprising 22-year-old, built a giant radio antenna from 400 feet of brass piping mounted on wooden posts. The antenna was mobile—it had wheels taken from an old Model-T Ford—and it was hooked up to an amplifier and a moving-paper recorder that would produce graphs of radio emissions from various directions. Day after day, Jansky went out to the potato field and trundled his outlandish contraption around in circles, hoping to determine the direction from which the static interference was coming.

Though he became ill with a serious kidney problem, Jansky returned to the potato field again and again. By 1932, he had learned that most of the static in question was caused by thunderstorms. But there was an additional, persistent hissing. This noise was loudest when Jansky aimed his antenna at a certain part of the sky. Jansky acquired a star chart. The mysterious hiss was coming from the part of the sky where the center of the Milky Way was located.

Light is a form of electromagnetic radiation. Visible light—that is, the electromagnetic radiation that can be perceived by the human eye—occupies only a narrow band of the entire electromagnetic spectrum. The rest of the

Radio galaxy NGC 1316, captured by the Very Large Array interferometer at Socorro, New Mexico, in 1985. The galaxy is emanating two massive lobes of intense radio energy. This spectacular display is invisible to optical telescopes.

Carl Jansky, the world's first radio astronomer, adjusts his mobile radio antenna in a New Jersey potato field. Jansky's pioneering labors revealed that the Milky Way gives off powerful radio emissions, but the significance of his discovery was downplayed by optical astronomers.

spectrum is taken up by what astrophysicists call nonvisible light—electromagnetic energy with longer or shorter wavelengths than visible light, including gamma rays, X rays, ultraviolet light, infrared light, and radio waves. Stellar objects emit visible light; they also generate some of the other forms of electromagnetic radiation, including radio waves. (*Everything* in the universe emits radio waves.) Radio waves cannot be "seen" by the human eye or by an optical telescope, but an antenna like Jansky's potato-field device can receive them.

Jansky's antenna was picking up emissions from a powerful radio source located at the center of the Milky Way. Jansky announced his discovery in 1932. It was treated as a scientific novelty and nothing more. Astronomers and astrophysicists brushed it off. The information was interesting, they felt, but essentially useless. A comment in the June 1933 issue of the *New Yorker* magazine summed up the general attitude toward Jansky's discovery: "It has been demonstrated that a receiving set of great delicacy in New Jersey will get a new kind of static from the Milky Way. This is believed to be the longest distance anybody ever went to look for trouble."

Carl Jansky felt that his discovery was far from trivial. He believed that he had opened a new window onto the cosmos. He suggested that information from deep space was raining down to earth in the form of radio waves. Instruments such as his potato-field device, he asserted, would allow astronomers to investigate a universe that had been invisible up until then, perhaps revealing some of the secrets of deep space; secrets that were hidden to optical telescopes. But it seemed that nobody was listening to Jansky. His bosses at Bell declined to let him continue his potato-field research and put him to work on other projects.

Somebody *was* listening, however. In Wheaton, Illinois, a suburb of Chicago, a radio engineer named Grote Reber had read about Jansky's work. Using his own money, Reber built—in his backyard—the first true radio telescope: a 31-foot metal dish that reflected radio waves to a receiver at its focus. It was a strange object to appear in anybody's backyard during the years of the Great Depression, and Reber's neighbors wondered if they had an authentic mad scientist, or perhaps a foreign spy, on their hands. Reber's behavior did not dispel their suspicions. He would return home from work in the evening, eat dinner, take a short nap, and then spend the entire night probing the sky with his radio telescope.

Reber's lonely vigils produced the first radio maps of our galaxy. (Radio maps are contour charts that represent the intensity of radio emissions from the areas of the sky being probed. They are drawn by recording devices connected to the receiver at the focus of the radio telescope.) In 1940, Reber took his maps and charts to astronomers at the University of Chicago. The astronomers—including Otto Struve, who would eventually become the director of the National Radio Astronomy Observatory—were intrigued. They wanted to see Reber's radio telescope, and a group of them traveled to Wheaton. Reber's mother was using the dish as one end of her clothesline, so Reber had to postpone the demonstration, but the science of radio astronomy had finally emerged from the shadows of obscure potato fields and suburban backyards.

During World War II, radio technology developed for military purposes was utilized by a growing number of deep-space explorers who called themselves radio astronomers. Even the most traditional and skeptical optical astronomers began to realize the importance and potential of radio astronomy. Just as Carl Jansky had suggested, information from deep space was indeed streaming to earth in the form of radio waves, and by the 1950s big radio dishes were ubiquitous. They tended to appear in mushroomlike clusters—two or more radio telescopes can be used together to form, in effect, one big radio telescope, a device known as an interferometer—which most often sprang up in uninhabited places such as deserts, where there was room for them and where there was a minimum of interference from terrestrial radio sources.

Because powerful radio emissions in deep space are often generated by objects and events that do not cause a corresponding emission of visible light, radio astronomers found themselves contemplating things—like the intense radio source at the center of the Milky Way first detected by Carl Jansky—that optical astronomers were unaware of. What appeared to an optical astronomer as an

(continued on page 73)

Deep Focus

The Jewel Box star cluster (NGC 4755), located about 7,800 light-years away. The bright orange object is Kappa Crucis, a star in the red giant phase.

The name of the first photoastronomer has been lost to history—perhaps it was an amateur astronomer or backyard gadgeteer —but at some point in the late 19th or early 20th century, somebody somewhere attached a camera to a telescope and obtained a gray, fuzzy image of a celestial object on a primitive photographic plate. By the 1940s, when pioneer photoastronomer Milton Humason assisted Edwin Hubble in photographing a Cepheid-variable star in the Andromeda nebula, astronomy and photography had become linked as two integral parts of the same endeavor. Over the years, improvements in cameras, lenses, filters, and photographic emulsions steadily enhanced the images captured from deep space. Hypersensitized emulsions coated on glass plates (manufactured by Eastman Kodak) are used at most of the major observatories today. These emulsions are treated (usually they are baked in nitrogen and then soaked in hydrogen gas) for hypersensitization to visible light as well as nonvisible light from the various segments of the electromagnetic spectrum. Some telescopes, such as the Hale 200-inch and the Keck telescope in Hawaii, are now equipped with charge-coupled devices, or CCDs. On a chip roughly the size of a postage stamp, as many as 64,000 silicon pixels—microscopic, light-sensitive cells—receive incoming photons (light particles) collected by a telescope mirror focused on a star, galaxy, nebula, or quasar. The photons cause the pixels to emit electrons, which are carried to computers via hair-thin video wire and reconstructed digitally to form images of the deep-space objects under observation. CCDs are as much as 200 times more light-sensitive than the photographic plates used by Hubble and Humason. Telescope cameras using hypersensitized emulsions and telescopes equipped with CCD cameras produce startling heavenly images such as those seen on the following pages.

*The Horsehead Nebula, set aglow by nearby
stars and excited hydrogen, and the dark nebulosity
IC 434. The brilliant star in the foreground is Zeta
Orionis. The strange "horse's head" is a dusty
projection from IC 434.*

The Trifid Nebula M20 (NGC 6514), womb of stars. Forty light-years across, the nebula is lit from within by newborn stars.

The Helix, or Sunflower planetary nebula (NGC 7293), an expanding shell of gas ejected by a star late in the red-giant phase. At a distance of about 400 light-years, the Helix is the closest planetary nebula to earth.

The Vela supernova remnant, nebulous remains of a star that exploded about 120 centuries ago. Shock waves from the explosion continue to ripple outward, causing interstellar gas and dust to heat up and become luminous.

Nebulae NGC 6559 and IC 1274-75; the
soft reds and blues of fluorescent hydrogen are
illuminated from within by young, hot stars.

The Large Magellanic Cloud (LMC), a small companion galaxy to the Milky Way. The LMC is 160,000 light-years distant. Star clusters and nebulae are splashed at random across its face, indicating that the galaxy is producing multitudes of new stars.

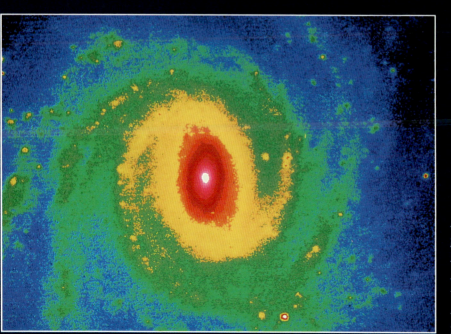

A color-enhanced photograph of the galaxy Arp 41 (NGC 1232). A typical spiral galaxy much like the Milky Way, Arp 41 is 65 million light-years away.

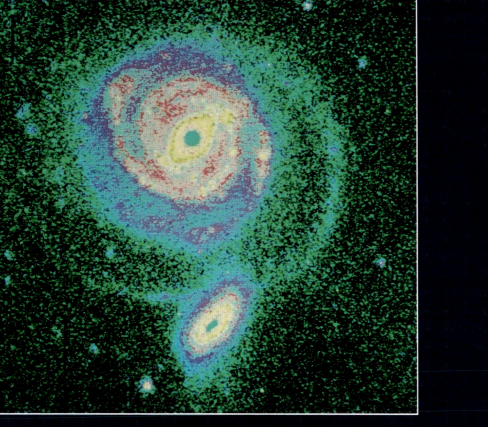

*Galaxies Arp 297 (NGC 5754)
and Wilson 31 (NGC 5755),
an unusual pair of interacting
galaxies.*

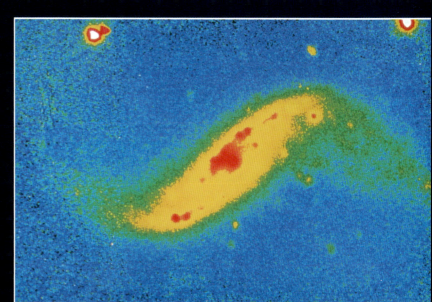

*NGC 3187, a spiral galaxy
with unfurling arms caused by
the gravitational influence of
a nearby, unseen galaxy.*

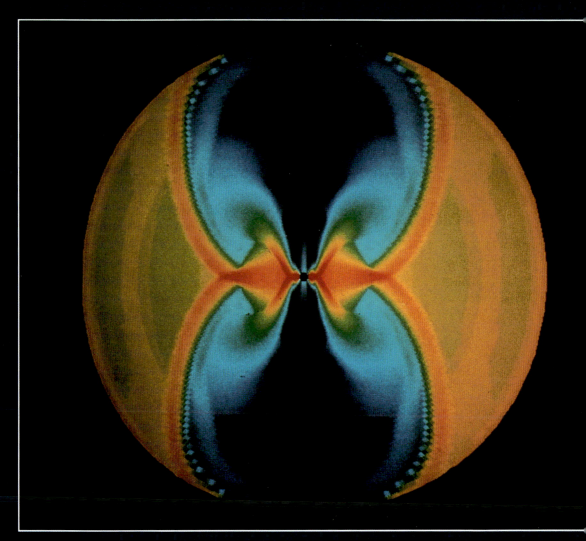

*A supercomputer-generated simulation of a black hole and sur-
rounding accretion disk. The black hole itself is at the center of
the image; the surrounding matter is the accretion disk, a swirl-
ing accumulation of gas, dust, and other matter, much of which
will be sucked into the black hole.*

Grote Reber, *who began his ca-reer as an amateur radio astronomer in suburban Illinois, stands before astronomy's first radio telescope, which he built singlehanded in his backyard, at a cost of $4,000, and then used to make the first ra-dio maps of the Milky Way. The historic telescope is now on display at the National Radio Astronomy Observatory in Green Bank, West Virginia.*

(continued from page 64)

unremarkable point of light, or what might not appear to an optical astronomer at all, might "appear" to a radio astronomer as a glaring patch of energy. Thus, radio astronomers rapidly acquired reams of vital new informa-tion about deep space; information that optical astron-omers could not have obtained.

In August 1967, Jocelyn Bell, a 24-year-old Irish-born astrophysics graduate student at Cambridge University in England, noticed something unusual when she analyzed the radio-emission graphs from the university's football-field-sized "antenna farm," which was made up of 2,040 interconnected radio antennas used to monitor deep-space radio sources. What Bell detected was a series of regular pulses of radio energy emanating from the direction of the constellation Vulpecula (the Little Fox). The unusual thing about the pulses was their regularity; a pulse occurred every 1.3 seconds and lasted exactly 0.016 of a second.

Astronomers had never encountered anything like this mysterious radio source. The signal seemed too precise and regular to be of a natural origin. Jocelyn Bell and her colleagues at Cambridge were forced to confront the unnerving possibility that they were receiving a signal of an artificial—and thus an intelligent—origin; a radio beacon, perhaps from an inhabited planet circling some distant star. Bell was flabbergasted. "Here I was trying to get a Ph.D.," she later recalled, "and some silly lot of little green men had to choose my aerial and my [radio] frequency to get in touch with us." The Cambridge astronomers dubbed the mysterious radio source LGM-1. (LGM stood for Little Green Men.)

Bell began spending her nights poring over the antenna farm graphs of other parts of the sky. To her amazement, she found other radio sources much like LGM-1, but in entirely different areas of the sky. Bell was relieved; these new radio sources eliminated the little-green-men theory—it was highly unlikely that several extraterrestrial civilizations hundreds of thousands of light years apart were all trying to signal planet earth in the same manner at the same time. But the mystery of the true nature of the objects remained.

A solution to the mystery was provided by the Austrian-born astronomer Thomas Gold, who was affiliated with Cornell University at the time. According to Gold, Jocelyn Bell's LGMs were rapidly spinning neutron stars. Neutron stars are among the most remarkable objects to be found in deep space. Their existence was first postulated in the 1930s by physicist Subrahmanyan Chandrasekhar of India and astrophysicists Fritz Zwicky (born in Bulgaria) and Walter Baade (born in Germany).

Chandrasekhar was interested in the fate of massive stars that ran out of nuclear fuel to burn. Applying some of the principles of general relativity as well as some of Sir Arthur Eddington's equations regarding stellar atomic structure, Chandrasekhar concluded that these stars would undergo a process of acute gravitational collapse. Taking the theory a step further, Zwicky and Baade proposed that the ultimate result of this process would be the phenomenon known as a black hole or a strange object called a neutron star. A neutron star is small—having a diameter of only 10 to 15 miles—and super dense; a smooth ball of compressed neutrons (subatomic particles). As a result of the powerful gravitational collapse it undergoes, the matter making up a neutron star is so dense that a spoonful of the stuff would weigh about 1 billion tons.

Thomas Gold, upon hearing about LGM radio sources, concluded that they were generated by the rapid rotation of neutron stars. The process of collapse that produced neutron stars, Gold explained, would cause a star to spin; as the star became steadily smaller and more dense, it would gain angular momentum and spin faster and faster. The end result of the stellar collapse—the neutron star—would retain the spinning motion. (Today it is believed that neutron stars can spin as fast as 1,000 revolutions per second.) The effect of this high velocity spinning on the neutron star's magnetic field would be the emission of regular, powerful bursts, or pulses, of radio energy. These were the LGM "signals" discovered by Jocelyn Bell. Their source, the spinning neutron stars, were officially dubbed pulsars, for pulsating stars.

When the existence of neutron stars (and black holes) was first proposed, many astrophysicists disputed the theory. Sir Arthur Eddington declared Subrahmanyan Chandrasekhar's ideas about the gravitational collapse of

(continued on page 78)

Event Horizon

Nothing in the history of modern astronomy has excited as much speculation and controversy as the object, or event, known as a black hole. The concept—for no actual black hole has yet been definitively located or studied, although there are now several possible candidates under observation—has provided endless imaginative fodder for science fiction writers and endless theoretical fodder for physicists and astrophysicists.

Black holes are one of the more exotic theoretical manifestations of general relativity. As formulated and elaborated upon by physicists Fritz Zwicky, Walter Baade, Subrahmanyan Chandrasekhar, Robert Oppenheimer, John Wheeler (who first coined the term *black hole*), and Stephen Hawking, among others, the standard model for the formation of a stellar black hole involves the collapse of large stars of at least one and a half times the mass of our sun. A star without at least this mass (known as the Chandrasekhar limit) will undergo normal cooling, expansion, and then contraction once it has exhausted its nuclear fuel. The gravitational collapse of stars below the Chandrasekhar limit will eventually be halted by what is known as the exclusion principle—resistance between the molecular particles within the star as they are compressed. This resistance will increase as the star contracts and will eventually become strong enough to offset and halt the gravitational collapse, stabilizing the star at the white dwarf or black dwarf phase. Stars above the Chandrasekhar limit will experience a more intense gravitational collapse; some of these will become neutron stars when their contraction is arrested by a variation of the exclusion principle.

For extremely massive stars, however, usually at least four to five times the mass of our sun, the exclusion principle will not be strong enough to offset the gravitational contraction; the gravity generated by the star's own mass and increasing density will overwhelm the exclusion principle. What follows is runaway gravitational collapse. With no internal force to stop it, the star will simply continue to collapse in on itself, until it reaches a point of infinite density and zero volume—a phenomenon known as a singularity.

The star has now, in effect, disappeared from the perceivable universe, like a cartoon character who jumps into a hole and pulls the hole in after him. What this process has left behind is a different kind of hole—a profound disturbance in spacetime, a region where gravity is so intense that nothing, not even light, can escape from it. Any object falling within the boundary of a black hole—this boundary is known as the "event horizon"—will be sucked into the black hole and will disappear from our universe forever.

What would happen to such an object as it vanished beyond the event horizon and into the black hole? Physicists have been amusing themselves with this question for years. What would happen, for example, if the object were an astronaut? Most physicists believe that the astronaut would be destroyed by the intense gravitational forces at play within the black hole, or would explode in a flash of gamma rays as he or she approached the singularity at the hole's core. Theoretically, an astronaut who managed to survive the passage would experience some very strange things, including acute relativistic time distortion, which, for example, would enable him or her to see, in a few brief flashing seconds, the entire future of the universe in all its detail. If the astronaut were to somehow bypass the singularity, he or she might then travel through a tunnel in spacetime—known as a "wormhole"—eventually being spewed out the other end of the tunnel, the so-called "white hole" exit, into a different universe.

Professor Stephen Hawking. Despite a 20-year battle with Lou Gehrig's disease, Hawking has become the most brilliant and well known theoretical physicist of our time. Hawking, the premier authority on black holes, commented in his book A Brief History of Time *on the difficulties of locating the enigmatic objects. Searching for black holes, Hawking writes, "might seem a bit like looking for a black cat in a coal cellar."*

(continued from page 75)

massive stars "absurd," even though Chandrasekhar used some of Eddington's own equations in his theories. Others felt that the existence of neutron stars was possible but that there was no way to actually detect them because they were too small and dark. But Jocelyn Bell had found them. Today, there are 450 known pulsars, and astronomers believe that there are probably tens of thousands of them in the Milky Way alone.

Many scientists had also concluded, back in the 1940s, that there was no way to detect George Gamow's cosmic background radiation—the microwave afterglow of the Big Bang—and that therefore the Big Bang theory could never be proved. But in 1965, the so-called "echo of creation" was finally heard. The discovery was made by deep-space radio astronomers, and, fittingly, it was made in Holmdel, New Jersey, not far from Carl Jansky's potato field.

In 1963, Arno Penzias and Robert K. Wilson, two radio astronomers and engineers working for Bell Laboratories, were preparing a radio receiver to probe the Milky Way for radio sources. The receiver had originally been developed to receive radio and television signals relayed across the Atlantic via the first Telstar satellite. Penzias and Wilson intended to improve its already considerable sensitivity and then use it to listen in on the galaxy. Appropriately, the receiver resembled a giant, antique hearing aid.

To the annoyance of the two radio men, the receiver produced an anomalous hiss—a tiny but steady whisper of radio interference that registered in the microwave end of the radio spectrum. No matter which direction they pointed the receiver, the hiss remained; it seemed to be coming from everywhere at once. Penzias and Wilson went to great pains to eliminate the static. They ruled out all known earthly and extraterrestrial sources of natural or artificial radio interference. They took the receiver apart—

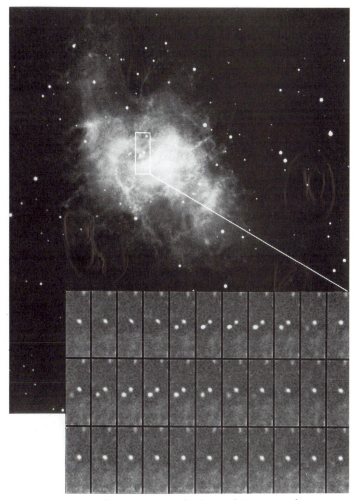

The Crab pulsar, located within the Crab nebula. The Crab nebula is the remains of a supernova that exploded 1,000 years ago. The panels on the right show the pulsar itself, which flashes once every millisecond.

some pigeons flew out—and cleaned it piece by piece. Then they reassembled it. But the "damn noise," as Penzias called it, persisted. Penzias and Wilson were embarrassed; they felt that their inability to find and correct the source of the "problem" would cast doubts on their abilities as radio engineers. They even considered not telling anyone about it.

Fortunately, they did tell someone, and through a most improbable set of circumstances, involving, among other things, a coincidental meeting on an airplane, Penzias

Dr. Arno Penzias and Dr. Robert Wilson in a photo taken in 1978, shortly after they received the Nobel Prize for physics. Behind them is the radio receiver that first detected the microwave reverberation of the Big Bang.

found himself explaining his problem to a Princeton University physicist, Robert H. Dicke. It so happened that Dicke and several of his colleagues, including physicist Philip James Peebles, were in the process of reviving George Gamow's theory of cosmic background radiation. The Princeton team had recently concluded that Gamow's afterglow could be detected by a radio telescope or receiver tuned to microwave radiation at a certain wavelength. When Dicke heard about the anomalous static that was plaguing Penzias and Wilson, he felt a powerful urge to go to Holmdel and check out the situation.

In early 1965, Dicke and two other Princeton physicists drove out to Holmdel to meet with Penzias and

Wilson and examine their data and the receiver. It did not take long for Dicke to determine that the wavelength of the mysterious radio interference was consistent with the wavelength he and his colleagues had calculated for the cosmic background radiation. On a cold, cloudy winter day, the five men stood in the New Jersey field with their hands in their pockets, looking at the big receiver with a certain awe, while Dicke explained to Wilson and Penzias that their annoying radio static was in fact the remnant of the explosion that gave birth to the universe. He told them that they had made the most important cosmological breakthrough since Hubble discovered that the universe was expanding. Wilson and Penzias looked at one another, not sure what to say. They did not truly comprehend the enormity of their discovery until the story appeared on the front page of the *New York Times* several days later. They eventually were awarded the Nobel Prize for physics.

"The Thing Was Exceedingly Weird"

If there is a single phrase that best defines deep space astronomy in the latter part of the 20th century, it is *lookback time*. Post-Hubble astronomers are acutely aware of the fact that the night sky is a picture window onto the past. These astronomers are as much travelers in time as they are travelers in space.

An astronomer peering at a distant galaxy through a telescope—or a child looking at a star from a backyard at night—is observing light that started on its journey to earth years, centuries, or even millions of centuries ago. Light from the star Alpha Centauri—at 4.3 light-years the closest star to the earth (aside from our sun)—traveling at 186,000 miles per second, takes 4.3 years to reach the earth; that light is 4.3 years old when it gets here, and has traveled a distance of about 24 trillion miles. Light from the star Ross 248, located roughly 10 light-years away, takes 10 years to arrive. That light is 10 years old when it reaches the eye of a child gazing up at it; the light is older, perhaps, than the child. As seen by an astronomer today, the light from galaxy M 31, located 2.2 million light-years away, is 2.2 million years old. That light started on its journey to earth 2.2 million years ago, more than 500,000 years before *Homo sapiens* first looked up at the night sky and wondered about the stars.

Quasar 3C273, the "quasi-stellar radio source" that first revealed the secret of these mysterious objects to astronomer Maarten Schmidt in February 1963. The line of light emerging from the lower right of the object is a jet of energy thrown off by the powerful quasar; the jet is 160,000 light-years long.

Consequently, the *source* of any stellar light—a star or galaxy, for example—appears to an observer on earth as it looked in the past, 4.3 years ago, 10 years ago, 2.2 million years ago, or whatever, depending on the distance involved. (Even planets in our solar system appear to us as they looked in the past, although their light, as compared to stellar light, is only minutes old. It takes sunlight about eight minutes to reach earth.) Indeed, the source of the light may no longer exist; a distant star may have burned itself out long before its light reaches earthly eyes. Thus, when a person looks at the night sky, that person is looking back in time. Telescopes are, in effect, time machines. The farther, or deeper into space an astronomer can see, the farther back in time that astronomer can see as well. Astronomers call this phenomenon lookback time.

Deep-space astronomers in the latter decades of the 20th century can be characterized as voyagers in lookback time. (It can be said that all astronomers throughout history have been travelers in lookback time, but none have been so aware of the concept—and so aware of the relevant implications of what they observe—as the late-20th-century astronomers.) Their odyssey takes them backward through a kind of cosmic time tunnel, through layers of cosmic evolution and history, as they observe objects that existed and events that occurred thousands, millions, and even billions of years ago. What have these voyagers seen at the far edges of lookback time? Quasars—brilliant objects that are believed to mark the perimeter of the visible universe.

The primary instrument utilized in the discovery and investigation of quasars was—and for the most part still is—the Hale telescope; it can be said that the Hale, with its 200-inch mirror, is the flagship of the lookback-time fleet. The captain of this fleet is Caltech astronomer Maarten Schmidt. Since 1962, the tall, cerebral Schmidt, in the words of fellow astronomer Jim Gunn, has cast "a long, thin shadow" over the field of deep-space astronomy.

Schmidt is the inheritor of the legacy of Hale, who was responsible for building the Big Eye; of Hubble, who first utilized that telescope to extend humankind's vision into extragalactic space; and of Hubble's immediate successor, Alan Sandage, who assumed duties on the Hale telescope upon Hubble's death in 1953 and continued Hubble's inexorable flight outward.

The quasar era began in 1960 with Caltech radio astronomer Tom Matthews, who was studying some of the more intriguing radio sources yet detected. These objects were compact but powerful generators of radio energy that had not yet been associated with a corresponding visible object. Matthews, having obtained exact coordinates for one of these sources—radio object 3C48—sent the coordinates to

Astronomer Alan Sandage first located a quasar visually in 1960, using the 200-inch Hale telescope. Sandage, who had been personally trained by Edwin Hubble, was nevertheless mystified by the object. "I tried very hard to identify the spectral lines of [quasar] 3C48," Sandage said, "but I was baffled."

Alan Sandage at the Hale telescope, hoping that Sandage might find the object with the 200-inch. Sandage pointed the Hale at the section of sky indicated by Matthews's coordinates and found an unremarkable-looking point of light in the Triangulum constellation. That evening, he subjected 3C48 to a spectroscopic analysis. The unremarkable-looking point of light had a remarkable spectrum. Sandage was baffled. "It was the weirdest spectrum I'd ever seen," he said. "The thing was exceedingly weird." According to his analysis, 3C48 "made no sense at all"; its spectral lines corresponded with none of the known celestial objects or elements. (Spectral lines include dark, or absorption lines, and white, or emission lines, which are revealed by a spectroscope among the array of colors in a spectrum. Spectral line patterns provide information about the composition of stellar objects.)

During the next two years, more of these mysterious radio objects were discovered and pinpointed visually. Like 3C48, their spectra were incomprehensible. They did not seem to belong to the familiar universe of planets, stars, nebulae, galaxies, and the other objects and groups of objects known to modern astronomy at the time. Astrophysicists around the world puzzled over their bizarre spectra but could not decipher the odd patterns of absorption and emission lines. Judging from their visible luminosity, however, most astronomers agreed that the objects were relatively small and relatively close, probably located within our own galaxy. Sandage thought that they were probably some strange kind of star. Astronomers, for want of a better term, began calling them radio stars because of the powerful radio energy they generated, until a NASA physicist dubbed them "quasi-stellar radio sources," or quasars.

The objects now had a name, but nobody knew what they were. In 1963, one of the many astronomers attempting to solve the mystery of the quasars was Maarten Schmidt. Born in the Netherlands in 1929, the year that

Maarten Schmidt, who finally solved the mystery of the quasars in 1963. Almost 15 years later, Schmidt was still shocked by his discovery. "Even now that we've been with quasars for years," he remarked in 1977, "we haven't recovered from the surprise. I still can't believe it."

George Hale first approached John D. Rockefeller with the idea of building a 200-inch telescope, Schmidt had joined the Caltech staff in 1959. (Schmidt had been living in Southern California for a while and was already quite Americanized when he came to Caltech; he was known to munch bags of Chips Ahoy! chocolate-chip cookies while observing galaxies up on Mount Palomar.) One day in February 1963, Schmidt sat in his office at Caltech, staring at the spectrum for quasar 3C273 on a small piece of film. Schmidt stared and stared at the odd spectrum. He stared so long and so hard that he got a headache. And then, suddenly, he understood. The spectrum was like a trick picture in which an object is presented in such a way that it remains hidden to an observer until it is pointed out by someone else who is already aware of its presence. Then the hidden object becomes obvious. So it was with the quasar spectra. The answer to the riddle, as Schmidt put it, "was right there in front of us."

The light of 3C273 was dramatically redshifted. It was redshifted so profoundly, in fact, that its spectrum had been, in effect, disguised. Astronomers and astrophysicists, operating under the assumption that the object was relatively nearby, had not even considered the possibility of a minor redshift, never mind the Hubble-sized redshift Schmidt had suddenly perceived. When the redshift was compensated for, the spectral lines of 3C273 indicated the presence of hydrogen and other conventional elements. But it was the redshift itself that now concerned Schmidt. He was beginning to feel somewhat redshifted himself, as if the nature and enormity of what he had just discovered were propelling his little office into deep space at near-light speed.

He was still sitting at his desk in his office, staring at the little piece of film, when his colleague Jesse Greenstein wandered by. Schmidt, pale and shaken, called Greenstein into his office and told him about the massive redshift in the spectrum of 3C273. The two astronomers began a series of frenzied calculations on a chalkboard. A redshift indicates that the source of the light in question is moving away from the observer. The degree of redshift indicates the speed at which the object is moving away. According to Hubble's law, in the expanding universe, the farther away a redshifted object is, the faster it is moving away. Thus, an astronomer can tell how far away an object is by determining its recessional speed, using the degree of redshift as an indicator of velocity. The redshift of 3C273, Schmidt and Greenstein soon determined, indicated that the quasar was receding at about 16 percent the speed of light, a velocity that indicated that the quasar must be about 2 billion light-years away, about as far away as any known object at that time. Breathlessly, the two men then retrieved a photograph of the spectrum of the first quasar to be observed—3C48. It had a redshift of 37 percent. Greenstein and Schmidt were stunned. 3C48, apparently, was 4 billion light-years away. All the previous assumptions about quasars flew out the window of Schmidt's office.

The quasar hunt was on, and Schmidt was the designated point man. With Schmidt leading the way on the Hale telescope, astronomers around the world began following the quasars, which led them into the depths of lookback time like streetlights receding into the night along a lonely country road. Quasars with unheard of redshifts were observed at estimated distances of 3 billion, 4 billion, 5 billion, 8 billion light-years from earth.

As they moved from quasar to quasar, the astronomers and astrophysicists tried to figure out exactly what they were. One of the first things they realized was that quasars are the most powerful radiators of energy in the universe. They are the brightest visible objects, but because they are so far away, they do not appear to be significantly brighter than other celestial objects. The fact that they can be seen visibly at all at such enormous distances is an indication of their unprecedented luminosity. They also radiate monstrous amounts of energy throughout the entire nonvisible electromagnetic spectrum. Most quasars are only about the size of a solar system, but a single quasar is brighter than a trillion suns and radiates 100 times the electromagnetic energy of the entire Milky Way galaxy.

Astrophysicists were mystified about the power source of quasars. How could such a small object generate so much energy? Various exotic theories concerning this question were proposed and discarded over the years, and for a while, all that the theorists could agree upon was that some almost unimaginably violent process was responsible. Eventually, the majority of astrophysicists came to the conclusion that

A radio image of a quasar blowing off a spectacular jet in the form of great blobs of energy. Astronomers have yet to determine the power source of quasars, although it is widely believed that gigantic black holes at the nuclei of these objects are generating the enormous amounts of energy as they suck in and swallow nearby stellar matter. A truly massive black hole may gobble stars as if they were cookies.

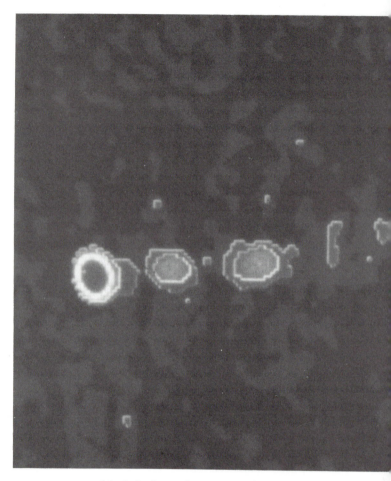

a supermassive black hole at the center of a quasar causes the prodigious energy output as it gobbles up surrounding matter, which spirals into the hole like water into a bathroom drain, throwing off gargantuan bursts of radiation in the process. Astrophysicists now speculate that a related phenomenon is responsible for the powerful energy sources detected at the centers of many galaxies, including the radio source—first discovered by Carl Jansky—at the center of the Milky Way. This link between quasars and galaxies may indicate that quasars are in fact the violent nuclei of certain types of galaxies in formation. Many astronomers believe that when they observe quasars, they

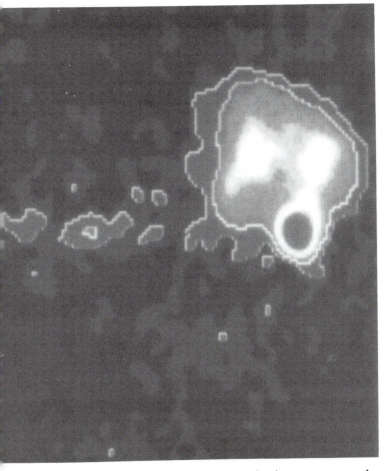

are seeing a lookback time image of galaxies in an early, high-energy stage of their evolution.

By 1965, Schmidt had found quasars receding at 80 percent the speed of light. By 1973, quasars receding at 90 percent the speed of light had been detected. These objects were an estimated 15 billion light-years away from earth. At this distance, the quasar population dwindled and, finally, died out altogether. Astronomers had reached what they called the redshift cutoff, or the red limit—beyond, there was only darkness. On April 8, 1973, a *New York Times* headline proclaimed: MEN REPORT SEEING EDGE OF UNIVERSE.

The View From Here

The astronomers of planet earth have come a long, long way since the days of Ptolemy and Copernicus and Galileo. There has been, to say the least, a radical change in point of view. Earth, once thought to be a cosmological centerpiece, is in fact a tiny planet gravitationally bound to one of the hundred billion suns that comprise the Milky Way galaxy, a pinwheel-shaped structure about 100,000 light-years in diameter and about 500 light-years thick. The great pinwheel spins, and the sun and its mascot planets are pulled along in one of its spiral arms—known as the Orion Arm—about 30,000 light-years out from the galactic center. The Milky Way revolves around the galactic nucleus, where some monstrous and as yet unknown object is situated like the head of an octopus, generating copious amounts of energy. Our sun and its planets have orbited the Milky Way's center an estimated 18 times so far—about once every 250 million years.

The Milky Way is a member of the Local Group, a cluster of several dozen gravitationally bound galaxies. The Local Group, in turn, hovers on the outskirts of the Local Supercluster, a conglomerate of thousands of galaxies of every imaginable shape and size. The Local Supercluster is but one of millions of superclusters aglow in the universal night. And yet, despite all this shining stellar matter; despite all these galaxies and clusters of galaxies and superclusters of galaxies; despite all these great, glowing metropoles of stars, the universe is anything but crowded;

A side view of spiral galaxy NGC-4565, a member of the local supercluster. Note the bright central bulge, which is packed with stars and harbors at its nucleus some as-yet-unknown energy source—perhaps a supermassive black hole.

it consists, for the most part, of black, empty space, and the vast, empty gulfs grow steadily larger as the expansion of the universe continues. Even so, this daunting knowledge of our less-than-significant place in a cosmos of overwhelming immensity has never discouraged humankind from its attempts to traverse the black gulfs and probe the brilliant celestial cities of deep space. In fact, it seems to have had the opposite effect.

In the years since astronomers glimpsed the visible edge of the universe, the exploration of deep space has intensified; indeed, it has become something of a global obsession, with an increasing number of countries around the world launching deep-space astronomy projects of their own, and many of these countries participating in joint efforts. An ever-expanding arsenal of powerful and sophisticated instruments has been trained on the heavens from points around the globe—and points just above the globe—in the continuing campaign to solve the mysteries of deep space.

The Big Eye still peers vigilantly into space from atop Palomar Mountain, but in Hawaii, an even bigger eye has opened. This is the $94 million Keck telescope, a joint Caltech–University of California project situated 13,000 feet above sea level atop Mauna Kea volcano. The Keck telescope boasts a mirror 10 meters in diameter that will collect almost four times as much light as the 200-inch Hale mirror. (Unlike the single-piece 200-inch mirror of the Hale telescope, the Keck mirror is made of 36 separate hexagonal mirrors fitted together and continually aligned and realigned by computers to maintain a parabolic perfection. The mirror will weigh only about one-third as much as the Hale mirror. Today's telescope builders agree that the Hale mirror is something of a miracle and doubt that it could ever be duplicated.)

Astronomers hope that the Keck telescope will allow them to see into the fiery interiors of quasars and thus solve the mystery of the quasars' source of power. The Keck is

currently considered to be the world's largest, most powerful optical telescope, but it will be eclipsed at the turn of
the century by the appropriately named Very Large Telescope (VLT). The $235 million VLT, which will have four
mirrors that will be able to work together as a single,
32-meter mirror, is under construction in northern Chile.

Today's radio astronomers are not hampered by the difficulties involved in building large optical mirrors, and thus
radio telescope dishes, known as reflectors, dwarf their
optical counterparts. The largest single-dish radio reflector
currently in operation is the 1,000-foot Aracibo radio
telescope in Aracibo, Puerto Rico. This reflector is built
into a gigantic sinkhole. Radio astronomers also have the
advantage of interferometry; they can use two or more
widely separated reflectors as a single, large, and in some
cases gigantic radio telescope. The most powerful interferometer on earth is the Very Large Array (VLA)—astronomers seem to be rather literal when it comes to
naming their instruments—located in the New Mexico
desert near the town of Socorro.

The VLA consists of 27 radio dishes deployed in a
great "Y" formation on the desert. The dishes are widely
separated, and each is 82 feet in diameter; thus the interferometer has, in effect, a 20-mile diameter dish. In
the 1980s and 1990s the VLA has been employed in,
among other things, the investigation of plasma jets (violent streams of energy, millions of light-years long, ejected
from the centers of radio galaxies and quasars), and mysterious objects known as cosmic strings, also known as
"cracks in the universe," which are believed to be potent
threads of energy that stretch across the entire universe.
Cosmic strings are incredibly thin but at the same time so
dense that they act as a kind of fracture in space-time.

One of the primary and perennial obstacles confronting
deep-space astronomers is the earth's atmosphere. Fogs,
mists, storms, clouds, overcast skies—and their ugly cousin,
smog—are the bane of the astronomer. But even on a

(continued on page 98)

*The Aracibo radio telescope
in Aracibo, Puerto Rico, is the
world's largest radio dish. It is
1,000 feet in diameter and 167
feet deep. The Aracibo telescope
is the primary receiver in NASA's
recently begun $100 million pro-
ject to probe the galaxy for radio
signals from extraterrestrial
civilizations.*

SETI: Only One Shaft of Wheat?

What are they really looking for—those who peer deep into space through powerful telescopes; those who monitor pulsars and scrutinize quasars; those who sift among redshifts and blueshifts; the probers of nebulae and the seekers of black holes? Although most of them would never admit it—and although most of them are probably not even consciously aware of it—the astronomers and astrophysicists of planet earth have always been engaged in a more fundamental quest than the search for new stars and quasars and the formulation of new cosmological theories. Their activities, ever since Galileo first pointed a telescope at the night sky, have been motivated by a more primal and deeply human need. In short, what they are truly looking for is company.

Until recently, primal needs notwithstanding, "serious" astronomers in general have scoffed at the idea of extraterrestrial life. But the knowledge of the size and contents of the universe acquired since the 19th century has greatly reduced the number of naysayers. Today, those who still categorically deny the possibility of extraterrestrial life existing somewhere in the Milky Way or beyond have come to sound increasingly shrill and defensive in their protestations, like the last of the flat-earthers or geocentrists. Indeed, given the number of stars—billions—in our galaxy alone, and the profusion of chemicals and elements in the galaxy needed to create life as we know it (not to mention life as we do not yet know it), many astronomers and other scientists believe that the odds *in favor* of extraterrestrial life in the Milky Way are something like 10 million to 1. As the ancient Greek philosopher Metrodorus wrote, "It is unnatural in a large field to have only one shaft of wheat and in the infinite Universe only one living world."

In the last two decades, SETI projects (SETI, or the search for extraterrestrial intelligence, is an umbrella term for all such endeavors) have shed their science fiction stigma and have come under the auspices of legitimate scientific programs and agencies. It has been fairly well established that there is no extraterrestrial life in our solar system, so serious SETI projects have from the beginning concentrated on the stars.

In 1972, NASA launched the deep space probes *Pioneer 10* and *Pioneer 11*. They were soon followed by the more sophisticated *Voyager 1* and *Voyager 2* deep space probes. After touring the solar system, these little spacecraft will leave it forever, embarking on a long, lonely odyssey into deep space. Each of these spacecraft has been equipped with a "message," in the event that they are discovered by extraterrestrials. This is highly unlikely, however. At their rate of speed, it will take the spacecraft hundreds of thousands of years to draw close to the nearest star, and they are but tiny objects, little bottles carrying little messages, adrift in a dark ocean of incomprehensible size.

It has been generally agreed upon that the best way to go about the search for extraterrestrial life is to listen for radio transmissions from the galaxy in order to pick up stray signals from intelligent sources or, perhaps, beacons directed specifically at earth. The first such project in the United States was undertaken by astronomer Frank Drake in 1960. Drake used the 85-foot radio telescope at the National Radio Astronomy Observatory in West Virginia to monitor radio emissions from two nearby stars resembling our sun—Epsilon Eridani and Tau Ceti. Since then, SETI radio projects have proliferated at a remarkable rate.

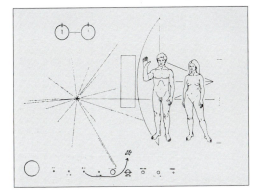

The message to extraterrestrials carried aboard the Pioneer *deep-space probes. Etched into a small aluminum plate is information regarding our species, the location of our solar system and the earth, and the launch date of the probe.*

Today, space agencies, the military, universities, and private citizens around the world are engaged in SETI programs of varying scope and sophistication. Congress recently allocated $100 million to NASA for a massive, 10-year SETI effort. Indeed, it is as if the entire world were listening. Unfortunately, our own radio transmitters are not powerful enough to broadcast signals to the stars, so the people of earth can only wait and listen, patiently, hopefully, and, perhaps, a little fearfully.

(continued from page 95)

perfectly clear night, the layers of oxygen, nitrogen, argon, and carbon dioxide that cocoon our planet interfere with incoming visible light; it is the atmosphere, for example, that makes stars appear to twinkle. The earth's atmosphere also affects the other forms of incoming electromagnetic radiation, interfering with them or blocking them out altogether. This is fortunate in some respects; if our atmosphere did not screen out harmful ultraviolet radiation and gamma rays, for example, there would most likely be no life (and hence no astronomers) on earth. Nevertheless, astronomers and astrophysicists, who must depend on incoming electromagnetic radiation to provide them with information about deep space, regard our atmosphere as a dirty window; a window that they are unable to clean.

"If only I could get my telescope above the atmosphere," many an astronomer has muttered since Galileo's day.

The Hubble Space Telescope is deployed from the cargo bay of the space shuttle Discovery *on April 25, 1990. Despite its well-publicized technical flaws, the Hubble telescope has made significant contributions already. In November 1992, it photographed what some astronomers speculate could be the turbulence surrounding a black hole.*

Today, in the age of rockets, space stations, space shuttles, and satellites, off-world astronomy is a reality, and it represents the future of deep-space exploration. ("If only I had enough money or political clout to get my telescope above the atmosphere," is the present-day astronomer's lament.)

NASA's somewhat infamous Hubble Space Telescope is to date the most ambitious off-world astronomy project ever undertaken. Designed as an unmanned orbital observatory in space, to be controlled, via radio and computers, by engineers and astronomers on earth, the $1.5 billion Space Telescope was boosted into earth orbit in April 1990 by the space shuttle *Discovery*. Astronomers had high hopes for the Hubble; it was to be the Hale telescope of off-world astronomy, transmitting back to earth images of unprecedented clarity. Great new discoveries and astounding revelations were expected.

Unfortunately, and to the profound embarrassment of all those involved, defects in the telescope's primary mirror severely crippled its ability to perform up to expectations. Accusations and recriminations flew, and for a while, the project seemed on the verge of becoming an outright fiasco. (One can only wonder what Hubble himself would have said about the episode.) Currently, the Hubble Space Telescope is still in orbit, performing limited duties—in the spring and summer of 1992 it was used to photograph an object called Arp 220, which is thought to be the remnant of two spiral galaxies that collided about 200 million light-years from earth. NASA has scheduled a repair mission for sometime in 1993; it is hoped the mission, which will be carried out by shuttle astronauts, will restore the Space Telescope to its full capabilities.

Off-world projects concerning the study of nonvisible and nonradio energy coming from deep space have been more successful. Satellites armed with sophisticated instruments—calling these devices telescopes and cameras would be an oversimplification—designed to collect and photograph ultraviolet, infrared, gamma-ray, and X-ray

In December 1990, astronauts aboard the space shuttle Columbia *used the Ultraviolet Imaging Telescope to take these ultaviolet photos of the spiral galaxy M81, which is located about 12 million light-years from earth. The NASA space shuttle program has proved vital to off-world astronomy projects.*

radiation arriving from deep space are currently orbiting the earth, and many others are in the planning stages. The International Ultraviolet Explorer (IUE), a joint project of NASA, the European Space Agency, and the British Science and Engineering Research Council, was launched into a high earth orbit in 1974. Since then, the IUE has orbited the earth once a day, investigating

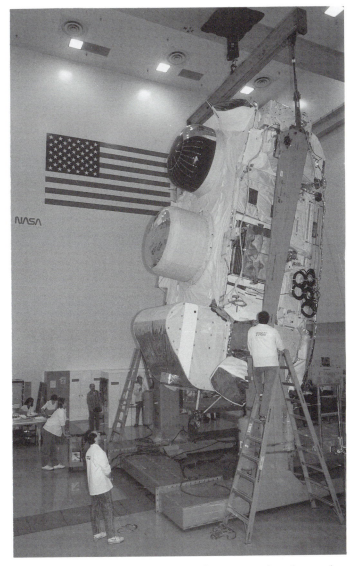

Engineers at work on NASA's Gamma Ray Observatory, which is currently in orbit. Gamma rays are usually produced by extremely violent deep-space events, and astronomers are hoping the observatory will provide information concerning high-energy occurrences such as gamma-ray bursters, supernovas, quasars, and black holes.

objects that emit large amounts of energy in the ultraviolet region of the electromagnetic spectrum, such as hot stars (stars with temperatures above 10,000 degrees Kelvin) and supernovae.

NASA's Gamma Ray Observatory was deployed by the space shuttle in April 1991. The Gamma Ray Observatory's primary task is to investigate the phenomena known as gamma ray bursters—thermonuclear explosions of an undetermined nature in deep space that release brief but intense bursts of gamma radiation.

The Space Infrared Telescope Facility (SIRTF), slated for a 1999 launch, will allow astronomers to see into the violent nuclei of infant galaxies in their birth throes, and also into the centers of more mature galaxies, such as our own Milky Way. Unlike visible light, infrared radiation emanating from the center of a galaxy is not obscured by galactic dust surrounding the nucleus. Infrared radiation thus provides a better, deeper view into the galactic center. The SIRTF may provide astronomers with new information about the powerful energy source at the nucleus of the Milky Way.

One of the most eagerly awaited astronomy satellites is the Advanced X-Ray Astrophysics Facility (AXAF), which is scheduled to be carried aloft and released into orbit by the space shuttle in 1997. Because objects—such as stars—being swallowed by black holes emit X-rays before they disappear into the black hole and out of the universe forever, astronomers hope that the sensitive X-ray detectors of AXAF will allow them to definitively locate one of those frightening and enigmatic *things* (for want of a better word to describe a black hole) for the first time.

And so the exploration of the cosmos goes on. The deep-space explorers have traveled via telescope to the very edge of the visible universe, and in so doing they have learned much about its contents, its origins, its size and structure, its physical laws, and its evolution. Indeed, they have seen and learned things that would make even Galileo's head spin like a pulsar. But perhaps the greatest achievement of the deep-space astronomers to date has been, to put it simply, finding out where we are. (Harlow Shapley deserves the lion's share of credit for this work; his contributions to deep-space astronomy are often overshadowed by Hubble's, but Shapley was the first true galactic trailblazer and cartographer.)

The Keck telescope, the world's largest, peers vigilantly into deep space from atop Mauna Kea volcano in Hawaii.

To ascertain the earth's location within the Milky Way and in relation to the neighboring galaxies and the Local Supercluster was a most remarkable and improbable feat. Indeed, drawing the galactic map from within the galaxy itself and then fixing earth's position on the map—*without ever having left the earth*—may well be the greatest single accomplishment in the history of observational science. This, then, is the most valuable legacy of the deep-space explorers: the universe is overwhelmingly immense and strange and complex, but at least we are no longer lost in it.

Further Reading

Boorstin, Daniel J. *The Discoverers: A History of Man's Search to Know His World and Himself.* New York: Random House, 1985.

Bova, Ben, and Byron Preiss. *First Contact: The Search for Extraterrestrial Intelligence.* New York: Penguin, 1990.

Clark, Ronald W. *Einstein: The Life and Times.* New York: Avon Books, 1971.

Ferris, Timothy. *Coming of Age in the Milky Way.* New York: Morrow, 1988.

———— *The Red Limit: The Search for the Edge of the Universe.* New York: Morrow, 1983.

Friedman, Herbert. *The Astronomer's Universe: Stars, Galaxies, and Cosmos.* New York: Ballantine, 1990.

Goldsmith, Donald. *The Astronomers.* New York: St. Martin's, 1991.

Hawking, Stephen W. *A Brief History of Time: From the Big Bang to Black Holes.* New York: Bantam, 1988.

Menzel, Donald H. *A Field Guide to the Stars and Planets.* Boston: Houghton Mifflin, 1964.

Overbye, Dennis. *Lonely Hearts of the Cosmos.* New York: Harper & Row, 1991.

Preston, Richard. *First Light: The Search for the Edge of the Universe.* New York: Penguin, 1987.

Ridpath, Ian. *Longman Illustrated Dictionary of Astronomy and Astronautics.* Harlow, England: York Press, 1987.

Smith, Robert W. *The Space Telescope: A Study of NASA Science, Technology, and Politics.* New York: Cambridge University Press, 1989.

Stott, Carole. *The Greenwich Guide to Astronomy in Action.* New York: Harper-Collins, 1985.

Chronology

A.D. 125   Claudius Ptolemy's *Almagest* establishes the accepted geocentric model of the cosmos

1543   Nicolaus Copernicus publishes *De Revolutionibus*, which proposes a heliocentric cosmos

1609   Galileo Galilei explores the Milky Way with the newly invented telescope

1623   Galileo publishes *The Assayer*, which attacks the Ptolemaic model of the cosmos

1633   Galileo summoned before the Vatican Inquisition; under threat of torture, he recants his heliocentric theories

1666   Sir Isaac Newton uses a prism to divide sunlight into a spectrum for the first time

1667   Newton builds the first reflecting telescope

1770   William Herschel begins to build increasingly more powerful reflecting telescopes

1802   William Wollaston invents the first spectroscope

1814   Joseph Fraunhofer improves upon the spectroscope

1837   Friedrich Bessel first determines the distance of a star, calculating that 61 Cygni is 93 million miles from the earth

1861   Gustov Kirchhoff and Robert Bunsen use a spectroscope to identify elements in the sun; William Huggins uses a spectroscope to identify elements in the stars Aldebaran and Betelgeuse

1879   Albert Michelson determines the speed of light

1908   The 60-inch reflecting telescope on Mount Wilson is completed under the direction of George Ellery Hale

1914   Harlow Shapley measures stellar distances with the 60-inch Mount Wilson telescope; using Cepheid variable stars and globular clusters, he determines the shape and relative size of the Milky Way and discovers that the earth's solar system is far from the center of the galaxy

1916   Albert Einstein publishes his general theory of relativity, revolutionizing physics

1918   Hale's 100-inch Hooker telescope is completed

1924   Edwin Hubble, using the Hooker telescope, discovers a Cepheid variable star in the Andromeda spiral nebula, negating Shapley's big galaxy hypothesis

1928   Hubble discovers that the most distant galaxies are redshifted, indicating that the universe is expanding

1929   Abbé Georges-Henri Lemaître formulates his Big Bang theory

1928–32   Karl Jansky detects radio waves emanating from the Milky Way, initiating the science of radio and nonvisible light astronomy

1935–1940   Grote Reber produces the first radio maps of the galaxy

1949   Unveiling of the 200-inch Hale telescope

1963   Maarten Schmidt determines that quasar 3C273 is profoundly redshifted

1965   Arno Penzias and Robert K. Wilson detect cosmic background radiation left over from the Big Bang

1967   Jocelyn Bell detects regular radio pulses from deep space, which are traced to rapidly spinning neutron stars, or pulsars

1963–73   Schmidt, using the 200-inch Hale telescope, determines that quasars are the most distant and powerful objects in the universe

1973   Astronomers glimpse the visible limits of the universe

1990   NASA launches the Hubble Space Telescope, which joins growing numbers of off-world deep-space observatories

Index

Picture Credits

Anglo-Australian Telescope Board/photography by David Manlin: cover (inset), pp. 65, 67, 68; Art Resource: p. 12; Courtesy AT&T Bell Labs: pp. 62, 80; Bettmann: p. 16; California Association for Research in Astronomy: pp. 70 (bottom), 71 (bottom); Courtesy the California Institute of Technology: pp. 30, 48, 57, 87 (photo by Bob Praz); Cornell University/Chris Hildreth: p. 95; Courtesy Corning Glass: p. 29; The George Gamow Collection of the Niels Bohr Library, American Institute of Physics: p. 58; Giraudon/Art Resource: pp. 14, 17; Harvard College Observatory: pp. 40, 43; Lick Observatory, University of California: pp. 50, 92; NASA: pp. 97, 98, 100; National Center for Supercomputing Applications: p. 72; National Optical Astronomy Observatories: pp. 32, 37, 54, 70 (top), 71 (top), 79; National Radio Astronomy Observatory: pp. 60, 73, 90–91; Basia Niemczyc: p. 45 (illustration); The Observatories of the Carnegie Institute of Washington: pp. 28, 38, 49, 82, 85; Roe/AAT Board/photography by David Malin: pp. 66–67, 68, 69; Roger Ressmeyer/Starlight for the California Association for Research in Astronomy: p. 103; Scala/Art Resource: p. 23; Science & Technology Division, New York Public Library, Astor, Lenox, and Tilden Foundations: cover; Courtesy TRW Space & Technology Group: p. 101; UPI/Bettmann: p. 77; Courtesy Yerkes Observatory: pp. 20, 26, 27, 34, 53

Terrance Dolan is a writer and editor from New York City.

William H. Goetzmann holds the Jack S. Blanton, Sr., Chair in History at the University of Texas at Austin, where he has taught for many years. The author of numerous works on American history and exploration, he won the 1967 Pulitzer and Parkman prizes for his *Exploration and Empire: The Role of the Explorer and Scientist in the Winning of the American West, 1800–1900*. With his son William N. Goetzmann, he coauthored *The West of the Imagination*, which received the Carr P. Collins Award in 1986 from the Texas Institute of Letters. His documentary television series of the same name received a blue ribbon in the history category at the American Film and Video Festival held in New York City in 1987. A recent work, *New Lands, New Men: America and the Second Great Age of Discovery*, was published in 1986 to much critical acclaim.

Michael Collins served as command module pilot on the *Apollo 11* space mission, which landed his colleagues Neil Armstrong and Buzz Aldrin on the moon. A graduate of the United States Military Academy, Collins was named an astronaut in 1963. In 1966 he piloted the *Gemini 10* mission, during which he became the third American to walk in space. The author of several books on space exploration, Collins was director of the Smithsonian Institution's National Air and Space Museum from 1971 to 1978 and is a recipient of the Presidential Medal of Freedom.